ROME *for ourselves*

ROME *for ourselves*

AUBREY MENEN

151 Plates, including 41 in color

McGRAW HILL BOOK COMPANY, INC.

New York   *Toronto*   *London*

For Philip Dallas

© AUBREY MENEN AND THAMES & HUDSON LTD 1960
PART VI NEW ROME © THE CURTIS PUBLISHING COMPANY 1960
LIBRARY OF CONGRESS CATALOG NUMBER 60-14528
TEXT PRINTED IN HOLLAND BY JOH. ENSCHEDÉ EN ZONEN HAARLEM
MONOCHROME ILLUSTRATIONS PRINTED BY BRAUN ET CIE MULHOUSE FRANCE
COLOUR ILLUSTRATIONS PRINTED BY JARROLD & SONS NORWICH ENGLAND
COLOUR ENGRAVINGS BY GILCHRIST BROS LTD LEEDS ENGLAND
ART AND COLOURED PAPERS SUPPLIED BY FRANK GRUNFELD LTD LONDON
BOUND BY VAN RIJMENAM N.V. THE HAGUE HOLLAND
41488

Contents

I WISH TO EXPRESS MY GRATITUDE TO MR PHILIP DALLAS, WHO WORKED with me in every stage of this essay and who generously placed his own illuminating research at my disposal: to Mr Ted Patrick for his active interest in reviving the art of the essay; and to Mr Harry Sions for his always sound advice. A.M.

Acknowledgments

Introductory Note

THIS IS A BOOK ABOUT ROME. IT IS, THEREFORE, A BOOK ABOUT history. I live in the middle of the twentieth century. I have seen a lot of history made in my time. I do not think much of it. I do not know anybody who does. This book is written with that experience in mind.

A book about Rome must also be a book about great men. I know a good deal about great men. They bedevilled all my younger years. Most of them are dead now. One or two turned out to be maniacs: others have been shown to be fools. One or two great reputations remain. But I suspect that a great man is a person about whom one cannot yet tell the truth. So it would seem to me. I am a child of my times.

Since I am writing about Rome, I shall also write about Christianity. I should say at once that I am a Christian believer myself. To be a Christian is a matter of faith. I have found that to be especially so when I study its history. Therefore, I do not recommend this book to pilgrims. Indeed, from my own experience as one, I do not recommend any book at all. In some circumstances reading can be a dangerous thing. Prayer is better.

I shall also speak about the classical Romans. Our forefathers thought very highly of them. They were held up to schoolchildren as models of character, although the most accurate description of their morals cannot even now be translated fully into plain English. Their political genius was profoundly admired, although the Romans themselves considered their method of Imperial government a subject for hilarity or despair. Their literature was the canon of taste, although everyone knew their historians were conscious liars and such poets as they had (they were very few) were admittedly sycophants, imitators or lewd. The art of the Romans was reverently copied, though they had none, being forced to borrow all of it from the Greeks. They were considered masterly engineers, although they invented nothing

7

in a thousand years. Their empire was considered one of the greatest achievements of civilisation, although it was run on a system of looting rendered merciful by corruption. I shall speak of the Romans, but with respect. They gave rise to one of the most powerful myths in history until Karl Marx.

Lastly, I shall tell of Rome itself: its monuments, its buildings, its ruins, its churches, its palaces, its apartment houses and its juke-box bars. This I shall do with pleasure, for the crimes and follies of mankind have produced the most beautiful city on earth. It is so beautiful that I live there.

This book, then, is not for saints or classical scholars, or for those who feel the past was better than our own times. It is for ourselves, we who live in the twentieth century: we who have seen everything, suffered everything and believe very little. For Rome, as I shall show, is our city, and the only one for us in the world, in which we, in a thinking mood, can feel at home.

PART ONE   *The Truth about the Romans*

1

It is reported that one day a Jesuit, who was a friend of
Pope Pius XII, said to His Holiness:

"Holy Father, I have been speaking at some length to a most learned
man. He told me that only one half of history was true. Does Your
Holiness consider that correct?"

Pope Pius XII, who was a learned man himself, thought for a while
before he answered. Then he said:

"Less than half."

When I had reached the age of forty-five, I had come to the same
opinion myself, although I could not speak with such authority. But
finding that I had some money and some time to spare, I made up my
mind to go and live in the city of Rome in order to test my conclusions.

There are two ways in which we can know what happened in the
past. We can read what people have written, or we can look at the
things they made. I had observed that historians relied very largely on
the first of these sources. I had also observed that while one frequently
found that two historians would agree as to what a document meant,
one could always find a third who would contradict them. I, therefore,
settled that I would, to begin with, study the second source, namely,
the things which men have made and left behind them. These are nowadays admired and preserved but, as I shall show, they are not often
closely observed. I chose Rome for my study because there are more of
these things in Rome than in any other city on earth.

For my headquarters I chose an apartment in the heart of the town.
It was halfway along a road that had the Spanish Steps at one end and
the great palace of the Borghese family at the other. It begins by being
called the Via Condotti, but it changes its name as it goes along. The
part in which I chose my apartment was hard by the palace of the
Ruspolis and it is called the Via della Fontanella di Borghese. It was
conveniently situated near the principal monuments; nearby was a place
where I could walk with my dog and even that was the mausoleum
of the family of the Emperor Augustus. I could not look out of any

9

of my windows without seeing some evidence of the past. I was surrounded by history. All I had to do was to walk out of my front-door and find out how much of it was false.

On my very first expedition, I came upon a most mendacious excavation, which in turn led me, within a week, to uncover a lie so big that I was moved to awe. But before I tell of this I would like the reader, who is going to accompany me, to join me in a short preliminary exercise, one which I had made some years before.

The most famous sight in Rome is undoubtedly St Peter's, and its most admired feature is its dome. It was designed by Michelangelo, and it is universally considered to be his best work. The line of the dome, in particular, is thought to be most masterly. On each of my visits to Rome, I duly studied it, and sought, in its design, to understand something of the great spirit of the man who had conceived it. Innumerable people have done the same thing, as you may do now by studying the photograph on this page.

As everyone knows, Michelangelo did not live to see the dome completed. When he died the reigning pope ordered that, under pain of ecclesiastical displeasure, no-one should dare to vary his design. The work was completed by two other architects, Domenico Fontana and Giacomo della Porta.

There is a good deal of their work in Rome and it struck me that their notions of design were altogether lighter and gayer than Michelangelo's. One day I jotted down some dates. Michelangelo died in 1564. The building of the dome was resumed in 1588. When Michelangelo died, neither of the two men who finished his work was over twenty-five. Twenty-four years had passed when they took up his work, twenty-four years in which fashions in architecture had changed profoundly. If the dome was really Michelangelo's I had to assume that these two men, already famous in their profession, humbly changed their style, obeyed the papal order, and reverently followed the long-dead master.

Do artists worth their salt behave like this? I doubted it very much. But then again, I saw that in this case it was possible. Michelangelo was an exceptional artist and the dome of St Peter's an exceptional commission. I re-studied the dome, as the reader may care to re-study the photograph. I made up my mind and you may find it instructive to do the same. Is the dome by Michelangelo?

I sought out his design. I found the design from which the latter architects drew as their working plans. I found that the designs were quite different. Michelangelo wanted the dome to be a hemisphere.

Michelangelo's design for St Peter's and the dome photographed from a distance

The other two, following the lighter fashion of their day, chose an ogival shape. A little more investigation on my part and I found out that Domenico Fontana and Giacomo della Porta made a cut-out sectional outline of the dome and laid it out on the floor of the still roofless basilica. Much as they admired the genius of Michelangelo, like true artists, they admired their own genius more.

They decided that they could do better and, in my opinion, they did. It is a fine dome. But it is not by Michelangelo.

To say that it is his masterpiece is, then, bunkum. To be moved by his genius, when one looks at it (as I was), is even purer bunkum. But the fact is that we find bunkum very much to our taste. We like the past to be dramatic. St Peter's was a dramatic affair. Michelangelo's death and the Pope's order to preserve his design is fine theatre. The fact that the Pope's order was never obeyed is a nuisance. So it has been forgotten.

This is not a failing peculiar to our own age. It is the permanent bias of the human mind and it is, for me, the principal fascination of Rome that here, walking about its streets, one can watch the human intelligence at work down the ages. It is, I admit, a procession of blunders and wickedness. But in Rome the climate is good, and the history of the human mind does not seem so very depressing, except perhaps when it rains.

I think that the best place to watch our minds at work down history is the Piazza of the Quirinal. In the middle of it stands an obelisk. On either side of this are arranged two colossal statues of nude men, each of whom is mastering a horse. On the plinth of one of these statues is carved in large letters THE WORK OF PHIDIAS. On the other a similarly bold inscription reads THE WORK OF PRAXITELES. Now these two immense groups were never buried. They were always known, even in the Middle Ages. At that time they were reverenced as among the most impressive relics of antiquity. They were regarded with such awe that, unlike so much else of ancient Rome, they were never broken up for lime. They were preserved because every learned person in the Middle Ages knew that Phidias and Praxiteles were two philosophers, who lived at the time of the Emperor Tiberius. Their knowledge was so profound that they were able to foretell the Emperor's future. Gratefully, he erected these two monuments over their graves.

It is an instructive story. We may smile at the credulity of our predecessors and reflect on our own. *We* know who Phidias and Praxiteles really were. They were two of the greatest sculptors of antiquity.

How we know this is another matter. Not a single work of either sculptor has survived. We guess that Phidias sketched the designs for the marbles on the Parthenon, though we are sure that they were carved by unknown sculptors. Praxiteles we know only through copies. This would not be so bad if it were not for the fact that all the copies are different. Nevertheless, we reverence their names. So did the Middle Ages.

There is one other interesting thing about the groups on the Quirinal. They are both very bad pieces of sculpture. They were probably hacked out by some copyist engaged in Imperial times to produce monumental sculpture as quickly, and as big, as possible. There were regular factories set up for the purpose and these statues would appear to have come from one of the less particular of them. The moulding is harsh and summary, the pose wooden and the animals clumsy. Yet, in the 18th century they were brought from where they were in the Baths of Constantine, set up, and deeply admired by generations of men of taste as masterpieces. They had a considerable influence on the history of art. Hundreds, perhaps thousands, of small-scale copies of them were turned out, often of a far finer design and execution than the statues themselves.

They were, and they are, part of the myth of Rome, which is one of the most treasured illusions of mankind. I shall now proceed to examine it.

2

ACCORDING TO THE ROMAN HISTORIANS, THE EARLY ROMANS WERE a people of exemplary character. They were fearless in war. They were frugal in peace. Sons obeyed their fathers and their fathers obeyed the laws. Wives were either chaste or sorry, because husbands were stern. Everybody ate simple food, wore simple clothes, and the men thought simple, manly thoughts. They behaved with gravity and decorum at all times, except during religious festivals when they permitted themselves a little rustic humour in honour of the gods. They despised art, philosophy and all neighbouring tribes, whom they conquered by force of arms and moral superiority.

It would be a surprise and perhaps dismaying if any such people had ever existed. Fortunately they did not. They were an invention. The Romans were not by any means a fanciful race, but most people can and do exercise a certain amount of creative imagination about their ancestors, especially if they think well of themselves: and, with the Romans, thinking well of themselves had been carried, over the

1 *The Apollo of Veii, made in vigorously-handled terracotta, probably stood on the roof of an Etruscan temple. The style suggests that it belongs to the 6th century* B.C. *It is now in the Museum of the Villa Giulia, Rome.*

centuries, from a pleasant hobby to a civic duty. Besides, they knew nothing whatever about the earliest Romans except what they could glean from a bunch of old wives' tales.

The Roman historians said that Rome was founded on the Palatine Hill by a hero named Romulus. He was, they said, sired by a god and suckled by a wolf. There is a lot more to the story which is as tiresome and incredible. I do not think it can interest anyone, save perhaps members of the junior branch of the Boy Scout Movement.

But the Romans themselves thought so highly of Romulus that they carefully preserved the house in which he was said to have lived, re-building it reverently whenever it fell down. It was on the Palatine Hill, next to the Palace of the Caesars, and in the place round which were built the first walls of Rome. The house fell into ruin for the last time when Rome itself was a deserted city. All trace of it was lost. Then in our own times, some archaeologists discovered the foundations of what might be a primitive house. Equally, it might be a cow-stall. They also discovered traces of a fire having been burned in it, which might be the primitive hearth, or, equally, might be the traces of a fire lit by immemorial tramps. But it was on the Palatine, it was near the Palace of the Caesars, and so, by that process of thought by which archaeologists so often find what they are looking for, it was decided that this hole in the rock was the house of Romulus. A roof was built over it to protect it from the weather, a notice was put up saying what it was, and the thing was done. My first expedition in Rome was to go and see it.

Relics were manufactured in the Middle Ages in much the same way. It would be difficult to take a religious relic today and persuade any large number of people to make a pilgrimage to see it. We are no longer in search of means to get to heaven. But we do go a long way in search of self-improvement. Tens of thousands of people, anxious to come as close as possible to the first Romans, climb the Palatine Hill and gaze, deeply stirred, at the hole in the ground.

As a matter of fact, I found that I could come so close to the first Romans I could count their teeth. To do this I went down the Palatine Hill, crossed the ruins of the Forum and entered a small museum. Practically nobody goes there, yet it is one of the most interesting places in Rome. The earliest Romans were lying all round me, in glass cases, and ready to be inspected when I had brushed away the dust.

They were discovered in the Forum in 1902–5. Looking for something quite different and more eye-catching, an archaeologist came upon a primitive cemetery. In holes dug into the rock, no bigger than a small trunk, were dozens of skeletons, some of them with their knees

2 *Nowadays we know more about the origins of Rome than did the Romans, who addled their own history with legends which they borrowed from the Greeks. This sarcophagus-cover showing a bride and bridegroom is the work of a people who shaped and, perhaps, founded the city—the Etruscans. It was made in the last half of the 6th century B.C. and is also in the Etruscan Museum of the Villa Giulia.*

drawn up to their chins, and hung about with necklaces, rings, bangles and lucky charms. They were the first inhabitants of the hills round the valley which later became the Forum.

The earliest inhabitants of Rome have been arranged in their glass cases exactly as they were found in their graves. Sand has been spread under their bones and the objects discovered with them have been set back in their original places. The skeletons are all bedecked. They wear collars made of stones, threaded together with lumps of amber. They wear bracelets made of curiously twisted wire. They are belted at the waist with metal plates, worked into a pattern and sewn together. They have rings, pins, brooches, and all sorts of other bodily ornaments in great profusion. Their jewellery is dulled by time and some of it has taken on the earthy tint of its wearer's bones. I found it, at first sight, a curious and macabre thing to see, but no more.

But one day while walking in the Via Condotti, I happened to look idly into the window of a fashionable and expensive jewellers. I saw a collar of sapphires and emeralds and I noticed that it was much in the same design as one that I had seen draped round the top of the spine of one of the skeletons.

I then discovered a thing which brought the yellow bones of the Romans to life. A woman who wore the sapphire and emerald collar in the jeweller's window would be considered to love luxury and display. A man who wore it—an Indian prince, for instance, of the old school—would love extravagant display even more. But the men and women of earliest Rome loved it so much that they could not be without it even when they were dead. For the amber beads, the intricate wire-work, the embossed metal plates were ostentatious luxuries, brought in some instances from distant lands. The earliest Romans were a people who were certainly dirty, often hungry, and who lived in huts furnished with a few earthenware pots. But they tinkled and gleamed with jewellery in every part of their bodies on which it could be made to stay put.

So the earliest Romans, far from being austere, were frippish. But we do not know what race the possessors of these bones and jewellery belonged to. They lived on the site of Rome, but they need not have been Romans.

Who were the Romans? Where did they come from? The Romans themselves said they originally came from Troy. The evidence for this was solely that a Greek historian, Hellenicus, said that the Trojan Aeneas had once been in Italy. Unfortunately, Hellenicus made up his history out of his own head, a fault shared by other historians, but

3 *This 17th-century painting represents the legend of the Romans stealing the women of a neighbouring tribe, the Sabines. Romulus, at the top left, supervises the operation. The picture is by the renowned French painter, Nicolas Poussin.*

4 *The Sabines returned to attack Rome in force to recapture their women. But they were several years too late, at least according to this picture. Their women had already set up house with the Romans and were so unwilling to be recaptured that they, with their children, stood between the two warring factions, and thus made peace between the Sabines and the Romans. In the background is Rome. The Sabines come from the left: the women and children are in the middle; and the Romans, with the standard of the wolf, advance from the right. The incident which, if it ever took place, could have been no more than a riot between neighbouring villages, has been turned into a fine work of art by the French painter, David.*

3

4

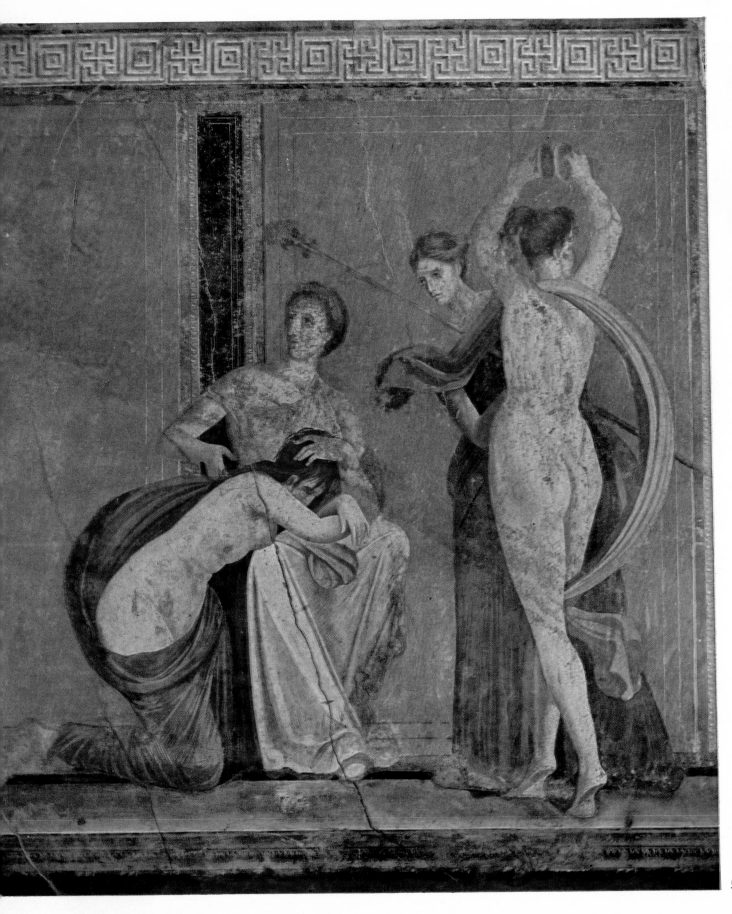

5

not so glaringly. His inventions, however, appealed to some Roman intellectuals of a later age who felt their fellow-citizens lacked refinement. The Greeks, at that period, were refined to the point of desperation. The story was considered handy. After a while it was considered probable: and when Virgil introduced it into a successful epic poem, it was held to be true. A longing to be thought refined was one of the most interesting aspects of the Roman character, especially among the upper classes. For instance, it was the ruling passion of the Emperor Nero's life, together with murder and incest. But apart from cultivated spirits such as his, it is doubtful if the broad mass of Romans ever took the story of their Greek origin very seriously.

Generally speaking, the Romans said they were Latins. The Latins were a people of mixed stock who were grouped round Alba Longa, a town in the hills overlooking Rome. It was held that Rome was peopled, under Romulus, by some Latins who had broken away from the hills. Because of their fortitude, their strength of character and their plain and simple way of living, they became irresistible soldiers and defeated all the tribes on the plain.

It is, indeed, possible that a hardy race of hillmen could descend and defeat the more lax and luxurious people of the plain. It has happened many times in history. If the Latins were a stern and hardy people, the picture that the Romans drew of their forefathers could well be true.

However, they were not. I discovered this one day when I was pursuing my studies of the men and women who had been buried in the Forum. They were an Iron Age people and I wished to find out more about that period in Italy. I went to the Ethnographical and Prehistoric Museum. It is a dreary, cluttered place on the upper floor of a palace, filled with a jumble of objects from primitive peoples all over the world, and case upon case of prehistoric implements, marked with yellowing labels, many of which had fallen out of place. It is, without doubt, the most depressing public place in Rome. Yet it contains one of the city's most dazzling sights. At the end of a long gallery, I came across a gateway of heavy bars, much as were used in old-fashioned prisons. Beyond it was an unlit room. I persuaded an attendant to open it, which he did with reluctance. He switched on the lights, and immediately I found myself in a treasure house.

There were vases of exquisitely worked gold and silver. There was an electrum breastplate stamped with a beautiful relief of little animals; there was a silver drinking cup covered in designs that are perhaps Egyptian, perhaps Assyrian; there was a gold cup with sphinxes for handles, and bronze tripods of elegant design.

5 *Detail of a wall-painting from the Villa of the Mysteries, Pompeii. The official, state-controlled religion of Rome was suffocatingly dull and few Romans believed in it. Instead, they imported more dramatic faiths from the Greeks and from the East. These were especially popular with women. We know little about them, except that they often included a symbolic rebirth of the devotee. This large 1st-century mural portrays some such rite, although no-one knows exactly what is going on. The woman with the small cymbals may be doing an ecstatic dance. The kneeling woman is being flogged.*

They had all been discovered in the tomb of Praeneste, a town near Alba Longa, and they were the possessions of a noble, perhaps a prince, of the Latin race.

Ten minutes in this treasure-house is enough for any person with imagination to reconstruct the life that must have been lived with and round these objects. The man who owned them was voluptuous and a show-off. He had a taste for rich living that amounted to vulgarity. Since this hoard of costly things was buried with him, it follows that his way of life was admired. The people of the Alban Hills, then, were by no means austere: or, if any of them did lead the simple life, it was for the same reason many of us have led it—they hadn't the money to do otherwise. Those who had, lived like lords.

It would be remarkable if they had done anything else. The tone of life in all northern Italy in the beginning of history was set by the Etruscans, a people whose major centres were to the north of Rome. The Etruscans left behind them innumerable tombs, so filled with evidences of their manner of living that the museums have not been able to show all that has been found. According to a tradition which there does not seem reason to doubt, Rome was at first ruled by kings. Not all of the kings existed, but some of them did, and two (or one who went under two names) were Etruscan by birth.

The next stage of my enquiry, then, was to visit the tombs that lie scattered in the countryside to the north of the Tiber and, once more, to visit the museums.

The Etruscans were known to antiquity, but it is only in the 18th and 19th and 20th centuries that their tombs have come to light. With the very first discoveries, our taste for the marvellous got to work. The Etruscans were labelled a mysterious race, and a great number of people think of them in the same way today. Unlike the other two museums I have mentioned, the Museum of the Villa Giulia, where their tomb-furniture is displayed, is thronged daily by earnest people who gaze, and puzzle. There is no puzzle. The mystery of the Etruscans is a piece of scholarly hokum, to which some present-day Etruscan scholars, I am happy to say, will no longer lend their names.

In the first place it is said that the Etruscans are mysterious because we do not know where they came from. We do not know where the Egyptians came from, nor the Greeks, the Dravidians, the Phoenicians, the Jutes, the Saxons, the Persians, the Chinese or the Aztecs or the Incas. Nobody knows where any ancient race came from, except the Germans who, every so often, are sure that they are Aryans.

6 One of the most beautiful pieces of sculpture in Rome, this panel is from the Ludovisi Throne, a Greek work made about 460-450 B.C. Generally described, till now, as the portrayal of Aphrodite rising from the sea, there is reason to believe that we have, in fact, a representation of some rite in a mystery religion similar to that shown in the previous picture. The bas-relief is in the National Museum of the Baths of Diocletian.

7 *The Roman Forum as it is today. It is the most interesting complex of ruins in the Western world, though repeated excavations have given some parts of it the appearance of a builder's yard. But the visitor, who can take a day or two to examine it, will find vestiges of every period of the long history of Rome, from the earliest tombs to the last column erected in Rome by an emperor. Here, on the left, is the temple of Antoninus and Faustina. Below it, a little to the right, is a low wall with a niche, built over the place where Julius Caesar was burned. A once-covered meeting-place, called the Julian Basilica, is in the right foreground. On one of its paving-stones can be seen a scratched design for playing some game—the Forum was notorious for its idlers. Beyond it are the three tall columns of the temple of Castor and Pollux, with the Arch of Titus in the background. Once the place where the fate of Rome was decided, the Forum became, under the emperors, little more than a shopping-centre, a stage for triumphs, and a place to gather gossip. Rome was ruled from the hill that rises to the right, the Palatine, which still carries the foundations of the palaces of the Caesars. Almost in the centre of the picture, in a line with the Arch of Titus, stands the Temple of Vesta.*

8 *Another detail from the Ludovisi Throne. Nothing is known of the meaning of this relief. There is a similar figure on the other side. Since that figure is clothed and this one is naked, it has been soberly stated by imaginative scholars that we have an allegory of divine and profane love. This is a pure invention, though a pretty one.*

Next, it is said that the Etruscans are mysterious because they wrote in a script which has not yet been deciphered. It has been admirably deciphered. The trouble is that the Etruscans were almost illiterate, and wrote nothing but names and two-or-three-word dedicatory inscriptions. They are mysterious only in the sense that it would be difficult to throw much light on the life of, say, Queen Victoria, if all we had to go on were her washing lists.

Lastly, it is said that the Etruscans are mysterious because the wall-paintings in these tombs show them everlastingly banqueting, singing and dancing, while the favourite expression in their portraiture is a happy, if somewhat vacant, smile. To a certain gloomy type of mind, it is perhaps mysterious that people should be cheerful. I do not find that it calls for any special explanation myself. But for those who need one, I would point out that the Etruscans did not read books, because they had no literature and, in my journeyings round the world, I have observed that a people without books is often as happy as a people without a history.

The Etruscans were, in fact, a cheerful and hopelessly unoriginal people. When their tombs were first discovered it was thought that they were astonishingly gifted artists. A great number of vases of exquisite proportions were found, all strikingly painted with human figures. For a time, the learned world rejoiced in having discovered a race of geniuses. Then it turned out that the vases were not Etruscan at all, but Greek. Metal urns were found, vividly engraved. These, too, were hailed as Italian masterworks until the urns from which they were copied also turned up in Greece. Great admiration was bestowed on the terracotta figures that reclined on the lids of the sarcophagi. Much was written about the mysterious smile that most of the faces wore. It was likened to the smile of the Mona Lisa, and much the same nonsense was written about it, until diggings in Greece brought archaic Greek sculpture to light. All the figures wore the same smile. Soon it became clear that the Etruscans either bought Greek art wholesale, presumably from commercial travellers dealing in the goods, or hired Greek artists, or had the more promising of their own artisans apprenticed to Greek masters. These artisans did commendably well, but added nothing of their own to what they were taught. Some of their clumsier attempts at copying have survived, and these statuettes have the charm of primitive or children's art: but nothing more. The Etruscans were not only a people without books, they were, to all intents, a people without creative artists.

Now, it is most unusual for a people who love beautiful things to be unable to make them themselves according to their own ideas. The Chinese, for instance, were surrounded at every turn of their daily life by objects of art, but they were all Chinese. Indian art is so indigenous as to be slightly repulsive to many people who are not Hindus. The Greeks invented everything in their art and borrowed nothing, unless it was from the Minoans who, as we now think, were Greeks in any case. There are very few instances of a people importing its art and its artists wholesale. Most civilisations find anything but their native art disagreeable. The British and the Americans, of course, imported virtually all their art, but it may be maintained that they, too, never really liked it.

The Etruscans, then, were exceptional in their lack of talent and their fondness for its products. It is a most important trait for this enquiry because it throws a great deal of light on the Roman character.

The Romans themselves admitted that the Etruscans taught them many of the arts of civilisation. The first temple on the Capitoline Hill was Etruscan, and terracotta figures made after the Greek pattern by an Etruscan stood on the roof. They learned many aspects of their religion from Etruscan soothsayers.

Now the Etruscans were the close neighbours of the Romans, who were Latins, who, in turn, resembled the Etruscans in their tastes and lives. The Etruscans, moreover, were perhaps the rulers and certainly the tutors of the Romans. It is likely, then, that the Romans, with such rulers and instructors, far from being the hard, tough, austere people that their historians loved to dwell upon, were, instead, a cheerful, ignorant, luxury-loving and wholly uncreative people who relied upon outsiders to bring them the cultivation that they hankered for.

The most sacred place in early Rome was the Capitol Hill. Here they built the principal temple in the city, dedicating it to three gods, one of whom was Jupiter. There is nothing left of it except, perhaps, a few foundation stones. But the hill today is harmoniously set about with buildings and courtyards. There are rambling gardens, rocks, and quiet. One can walk, think, and see nothing ugly. I spent many hours there, with a book. Soon I was able, in my mind's eye, to see the first of the temples that stood there, the place to which every Roman must have come, to which his thoughts turned in time of trouble or rejoicing, and which he looked up at as the heart of his city.

I was able to do this because Pliny, Ovid and Dionysius of Halicarnassus have left us descriptions of it. Moreover, from these we know that it was a temple in the Etruscan style, and many of these have been excavated. Indeed, so much is known about this sort of temple

9 *Part of the large wall-painting known as the Aldobrandini Marriage, since it represents a nuptial ceremony. It was found on the Esquiline Hill in 1605. It is, like all Roman art, a copy. The original Greek painting must have been done in the 4th or 3rd centuries* B.C. *In the Vatican Museum.*

10

nowadays that I may have a better impression of the original temple than Julius Caesar himself, who only had historians and traditions to go on.

It was large, almost square, and it was built of wood. Columns made up a deep portico and supported a steep roof. It was decorated with a vast profusion of terracotta plates, masks, gargoyles and floral panels. On the roof stood a quadriga, also of terracotta, and all the decorations were lavishly and brightly painted. To judge from the statuary that has been found near Rome of the same period, the artists who made the temple were thoroughly Greek in spirit and masterly in their skills. Livy, forgetting for once his picture of the austerity of his ancestors, says that the builders and decorators were brought in from all Etruria. It must have been a bold, gay and ebullient shrine, and it must have been very expensive. Temples are paid for out of the pockets of the worshippers. This one, certainly, could not have been put up by plain-living, dour and puritanical men with their roots in the soil.

On the contrary, it was the temple of a people who were so fond of pomp, circumstance and luxury in their ceremonial life that they had to be kept within the bounds of reason by law. The grandest ceremony in Rome was the funeral of the head of a family. Not only all his relatives walked in his procession, but also his ancestors, represented by masked figures who dressed and acted in the ancestors' manner. Laws were passed limiting the expense of these shows, forbidding, in particular, such lavish displays of wealth as burning the dead man in frankincense and providing the mourners with wreaths of gold to wear on their heads.

The Roman historians quoted such laws as evidence of the simplicity of manners in Rome and later historians have followed them. But it seems to me that they prove precisely the reverse.

According to one legend in the history of Rome, the Etruscans were driven out of Rome and, instead of a king, a combination of Latin families ruled the city. But there is no evidence that the Etruscan influence stopped. Indeed, such things as we have dug up suggest that it flourished. By the time that the Romans emerge into the light of convincing (if not wholly trustworthy) history, they have sunk so far into voluptuous habits that a puritan reaction has set in. Cato, the Censor, spent a great deal of his energies in reforming the manners and habits of his fellow-citizens. I have room here for only one instance of how far they had gone along the primrose path. One of his laws attempted to limit the buying of pretty slave boys to turn them into pampered favourites. The main objection to the practice was, it would appear,

10 *The mosaic of the drinking doves found in Hadrian's Villa in 1737, and one of the most celebrated of its kind. It is a copy of a lost painting by Sosos, mentioned by Pliny as being very fine. Each square inch of the mosaic contains over sixty pieces of coloured stone. It is now in the Capitoline Museum.*

the astronomical prices that the boys were fetching. Cato, himself, led a frugal life and kept a stern eye on his family, except when he got drunk. He lived very much in the manner that his ancestors were supposed to have lived.

But even he had a touch of the real Roman. In his old age, he fell for the charms of a slave woman, with whom his conduct was so scandalous that his son bullied him into dropping her. Deprived of one pleasure, he walked out into the Forum and provided himself with another, in the shape of the very young daughter of one of his clerks. In his defence—if any defence is really needed—it may be said that she had not cost anything to buy. For all that, it was a precipitous descent from the high ideals of a true Roman that Cato had hammered into his listeners' and readers' heads for a lifetime. It is significant that nobody seemed unduly surprised and his reputation as a great Roman did not suffer in the least. As a Roman, he did as the Romans did, and soundly berated them for it—a combination that was dear to the Roman heart, and still is. Cato drunk and Cato sober were, respectively, what the Romans hoped they had been, and what they knew they were.

They wanted to believe that they had come from an exceptionally stern and frugal stock because (in my opinion) they were imperially-minded. One way of obtaining luxuries that you cannot make yourself is to find somebody who has got them, knock him down, and rob him. The Romans were very successful at doing this. They were constantly at war with their neighbours, and by and large they came out on the winning side.

The Romans liked to think, therefore, that there was something in their blood which made them born fighting men and the best the world had seen. The truth is that, when they relied upon themselves to do their own fighting, they were not spectacularly triumphant soldiers. The Italian peninsula, including Sicily, was made up of provincial towns, petty principalities and near-barbarian tribes. It took the Romans a hundred and twenty-one years to bring this conglomeration under their sway. This may be contrasted with the onset of the Arabs, who conquered the Arabian peninsula, the Persian Empire and Egypt in the astonishingly short time of thirty years, dating the beginning of their expansion from the Hegira. Later, the Roman Empire expanded with greater ease. But, by then, the army was largely made up of foreigners, fighting for pay. Julius Caesar, in his own report of his campaigns, shows how difficult the legions found it to put down insurrections of ill-armed, disunited barbarians whose one notion of

11 *The head of an Egyptian princess or, perhaps, of a Roman girl with a fancy to be shown as an Egyptian. The Romans snapped up foreign ways and cultures as eagerly as an impressionable tourist does today. Cleopatra (of whom this was for long supposed to be a portrait on no grounds whatever) produced a wave of fashion for Egyptian things in Rome. In the Capitoline Museum.*

tactics was to dash, bellowing, from ambush in the woods. There is no doubt he exaggerated the difficulties in order to increase his own fame, as do all generals in their memoirs. But it is noteworthy that he thought his readers would be willing to believe him. Nor does the history of the Roman wars against Hannibal give us the impression of an invincible soldiery. There is none of the astonishing impetus that strikes one in following the campaigns of Alexander, nor the long-headedness of Napoleon's conquests in Italy. It is possible that the Romans were not, at heart, a martial people, such as the Spartans were. Their daily life, apart from the myth they built up about themselves, does not suggest it. Nor would this prevent them winning wars and founding an empire, even apart from the fact that they did it largely with hired labour. The Germans are a military people. The French love military glory. The British despise their regular soldiers and the Americans are the most unmilitary people in history. But the Germans can only beat the French. The French can beat nobody, while the Americans have never lost a war: and the British, in modern times, have never lost one either, except when they fought the Americans.

The object of all empires is theft, whether it be through taxes, concessions or plain looting. Most thieves think stealing is clever, but the Romans, when their larceny began to embrace all the nations of the Mediterranean, began to feel that robbery on such a scale had a certain moral grandeur. The British, who put together the only other empire that can be compared with that of Rome, thought much the same thing. It became convenient to the Romans to think of themselves as a superior people, marked out by destiny to rule the world. The trouble was that it was difficult to point out just where their superiority lay. It was unsafe to say that it lay in their paid legionaries. The legionaries said it for themselves, vociferously, and became increasingly inclined to march on Rome to force their point of view on the citizens. It could not be said that it lay in their culture, because they enthusiastically borrowed it all from the nations they conquered. They could not claim any particular merit in their political institutions, because they prostituted them to the rule of autocrats as soon as their empire was fully established. There was nothing left but to put it down to their character.

But, by the time that Caesar overthrew the republic, this had become manifestly absurd. Riches were pouring into Rome from all quarters, and the Romans set themselves to a dissipated enjoyment of them. The real Roman character was that of the vulgar, greedy, newly-rich, unrestrained by morals or religion. It therefore became

12 *The head of what is called the Apollo of the Tiber. The statue was found some seventy years ago in fragments in the River Tiber, close to the Palatine Hill. It is of Greek workmanship and it is thought that it was carved during the 5th century* B.C. *This masterpiece of the sculptor's art is in the National Museum of the Baths of Diocletian.*

33

necessary to invent a new character, more convincingly superior to that of their defeated subjects. This was done with a will: orators, historians, poets and writers of moral essays all played their part with vigour. Only two classes of men stood aside: the writers of comedies, who could not make people laugh with fairy-tales, and the emperors, who had to know the truth about the Roman character or be assassinated at the orders of someone who did. It is in the plays of Terence and Plautus, and in the sayings of the emperors (to say nothing of their actions) that we can best see what the Roman character was really like.

Public officers were regularly elected by wholesale corruption. The invented Romans, therefore, had to be men whose stern sense of duty forbade the taking of bribes. Romans spent whole days in gourmandising and lechery. They had, therefore, to be described as a people of temperate habits, chaste from respect for the laws and the gods. The torrent of wealth, much of it in the form of grain, was ruining the agricultural economy of the peninsula: absentee landlords were the rule. The mythical Roman, as a result, was devoted to hard work, particularly husbandry. The citizenry, from the Senate downwards, was pusillanimous and went in terror of the soldiers, whom they kept, whenever possible, away from the capital, with the exception of the Pretorian Guards, before whose swords and shouts they trembled. The superior Roman was, then, stalwart, fearless, a taker of hard blows and a giver of even harder ones. He was preferably well-decorated with the scars of old wounds. He loved hard exercise, blunt soldierly language, obedience and manly comradeship. Rome had enslaved itself to god-emperors. The Roman character, it followed, had to be imprinted with an ineradicable love of liberty. A nation of such people would be held by all as worthy to rule the world—*ergo*, that was what the Romans were.

The chief propagators of this myth were cultivated men. They were well aware of the growing swinishness of their fellow-citizens and, as I have said above, they tried to stem it. They attempted to import refinement, along with the wealth, and they chose Greece as its source. The ideal Roman they had invented would have no use for Greek things, but that did not bother them. They, after all, knew that no such Roman existed, even if they persuaded themselves that he had existed in the past. But among the things they imported was Greek philosophy, and in particular the doctrines of the Stoa. Stoic thinking was, in Greece, an elaborate chain of reasoning about man's relation to nature. The arguments of the Greeks led them to believe that the perfect man would hold that only virtue was good, and virtue con-

13 *The Arch of Titus in the Roman Forum was erected in honour of the Emperor to commemorate the capture of Jerusalem in 70 A.D. Built in the 1st century, it was used as a fortress in the Middle Ages and restored by Valadier in the 19th century. The Sacred Way began here. Inside the arch is a relief showing Romans carrying the seven-branched candlestick and other sacred objects from the Temple of Jerusalem. They are part of a triumphal procession.*

14 *The Colosseum. Built in 72 A.D., it was finished in the year 80. It seated 50,000 spectators. A cross inside reminds the visitor that for centuries it has been a pious belief that it was the site of the martyrdom of early Christians. There is no evidence at all that this is true.*

13

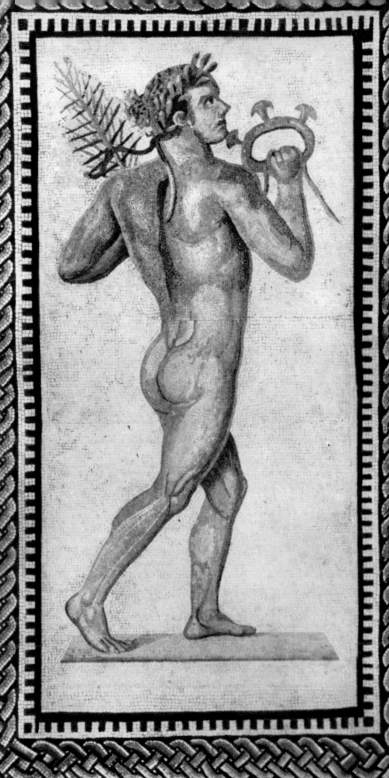

sisted in living as much in harmony with nature as possible. It followed that he would despise pleasure and equally despise pain, wealth, fame and the like, because he knew that they could not add to his happiness: nor could poverty or failure detract from it. His contentment of mind depended entirely and solely upon the exercise of virtue.

The Greeks at the time of the Roman conquest did not lay much stress on these bleak conclusions, since they were a people, even those of them who were philosophers, who were avid for fame, anxious for riches, and as put out by pain as any man. But the perfect Stoic greatly resembled the perfect Roman. As a consequence, the intelligentsia of the Empire seized upon the Stoic philosophy, and brought over Greek professors of it in large numbers. These, adapting themselves happily to their new listeners, gave lectures on the ideal man to rapt audiences who gratefully saw their own picture of the true Roman being given intellectual respectability from the fount of refinement and culture itself. The myth of the Roman character had made the grade.

A good while later, a Roman emperor with a turn for philosophy tried to live the ideal Stoic life and to deal with real Romans at the same time. He wrote down his thoughts about his experiences. As might be expected, the *Meditations* of Marcus Aurelius, along with *Ecclesiastes,* has been the favoured reading of disillusioned people for centuries.

But let me leave books and philosophers and return to the things which I saw in Rome. The ruins of classical Rome are numerous and often very large. But many find them disappointing. I did, until I understood what the Romans were really like. Then I found them full of interest.

The ruins of classical Rome are disappointing because they are not *classical* at all. We have all been taught what that word means. A classical thing is restrained. The ruins of Rome are flamboyant. Whatever is classical is subtly proportioned. The proportions of a building such as the Colosseum, are as subtle as those of a Greenland whale. The classical is that which fits its purpose, and no more than fits. The ruins of the Baths of Diocletian and Caracalla, the arches of the Basilica of Maxentius, the ruins of the palaces of the Caesars vaunt, sprawl and gesticulate. They are grandiose. In the classical world, man is the measure of all things. The columns put up by Trajan and Marcus Aurelius might have been whittled by fifty-foot giants, and need scaffolding to be seen properly.

But Rome was built for the most part by men who had no classical education. It was erected by parvenus, by multi-millionaires in the

15 *A bronze statue of a pugilist in repose, now in the National Museum of the Baths of Diocletian. It is signed by the Athenian sculptor, Apollonius. The boxer, wounded in the face, is resting between bouts. He fights with knuckle-dusters of heavy metal. This sport, like throwing criminals to wild animals, was uninhibited by any rules. The pugilists merely battered each other as hard as they could. Since such athletes were expensive to buy (rich men kept teams of them) and often enjoyed long careers, it is not unnatural to suppose that the sport was about as honest as all-in wrestling. Nevertheless, it was much enjoyed by the sporting public of Rome which, by imperial orders, included every citizen.*

16 *A mosaic from the Baths of Caracalla made in the 3rd century A.D. It is now to be found in the Pagan Museum of the Lateran and shows muscle-men, probably arena professionals, and their trainer.*

manner of William R. Hearst, by political adventurers, peculators, courtiers, imperial lunatics and patrons of the arts. Once that is remembered, the ruins come alive. The Forum of Augustus, of Caesar and of Trajan were not put up as models for young architects. They were meant to astound. And, with a little study, a plan and some imagination, they still do. The Baths of Diocletian were not put up to provide the Romans with a sound mind in a healthy body. They were built to remind the Romans that they were ruled by the richest man in the world—so rich, indeed, that he could afford to build them and not trouble, for years, to come to Rome to see how his money was being spent.

The most evocative place that I found in my walks in ancient Rome is a room in the pagan section of the Lateran Museum. It sums up what the Romans were really like. On the wall is a vast mosaic of hideously ugly muscle-men, heroes of the brutal sports of the arena. On the floor is another mosaic, wittily composed for a great dining-room. The artist, observing that Romans when dining made a disgusting mess of the floor by throwing food on it, has decorated the floor with pictures of the débris of a sumptuous banquet. Romans loved coarse pleasures and they had the money to buy them. They even had the money to portray them, for all time, in mosaic.

The ruins of Rome should be studied with this in mind. They can be a trap for the unwary, as deceptive as the Michelangelo dome. There is, for instance, a famous view of the Forum from the Capitoline Hill. There is a prospect of ruins and columns, set off in the foreground by the Temple of Saturn, one of the most celebrated and the most complete of all the monuments. Generations of visitors, whose aesthetic sensibilities have been stirred up by the thought of Rome, have gazed at this view and drunk in its architectural beauties. I do not say it is not beautiful. But I would like to point out that some of the columns of the Temple of Saturn are upside-down.

17 *The largest and best preserved of all the important roofed buildings of antiquity, the Pantheon was first built in 27 B.C. by Marcus Agrippa, but the portico shown in this picture was built by Hadrian. The roof was once covered in gilded bronze tiles. When the pagan religion was officially abolished the Pantheon was closed. It was then twice despoiled, once by the barbarians and once by the Christians. The barbarians stripped its interior and the Christian Emperor Constans II took away its bronze roof, in spite of the fact that it had, by then, been made into a church. The 17th-century architect, Bernini, restored this portico, which had then fallen into bad disrepair. It is now in a remarkably good state of preservation, and the interior cannot be very far from what it looked like under Hadrian. The outside, which today is brickwork, was originally covered with white stucco.*

17

PART TWO   *Commonsense at last*

1

NOW, WHEN I SAW THE TEMPLE OF SATURN WITH ITS UPSIDE-DOWN columns, it was borne in upon me that people who could knock together such a job and let it stand, could not be deeply devout.* I, therefore, reviewed with a more critical eye what I knew about the faith of the Romans, and I sought out more facts. This is the result.

The pagan Romans had two main religions: that of their forefathers and the one that, later, their emperors imposed upon them. It may be said, briefly, that the second could only have been swallowed by a people who were prepared to believe the first. Intelligent Romans believed neither of them.

The religion of the Romans of the Republican era consisted in believing that there were gods or geniuses, who were responsible for every separate thing in the devotee's daily round. Before anything could be done, the proper god, from this horde of deities, had to be propitiated, like a civil servant in some bureaucratic state. It was no easy matter.

Let us take, for instance, a baby. Should his parents wish to do the best they could for him, they had to take care that six separate deities were happy. Cunina watched over his cradle; Rumina taught him to take the breast, Educa and Potina, working in harness, made him eat and drink, Fabulinus made him talk while Statulinus was responsible for keeping him upright or, if neglected, for letting him fall flat on his face.

An ancient inscription (The Acts of the Arval Brothers) gives another instance. In this case a fig-tree had grown on a roof. It was not sufficient—it was not even wise—to take an axe to it. First Deferunda was called upon to assist in taking it away, Coinquenda presided over the chopping up, and Adolenda burned it.

Agriculture was attended by a platoon of celestial busybodies. Vervactor's concurrence was needed for the first ploughing, Redarator for

18 *The dome of the Pantheon is one of the most beautiful and satisfactory ever erected. Its width is equal to its height from the floor, a proportion which may account for its success. The other details of its construction are still not known but architects are agreed that, given Roman resources, its erection was not unduly difficult. It was the design that called for genius of a high order.*

* The error occurred during a restoration made in the second half of the 3rd century A.D.

the second, Imporcitor for the harrowing, Insitor for the sowing, while Oberator, under persuasion, blessed the dung. The chiefs of this agricultural department were Tellus and Ceres, to whom bribes had to be rendered in the shape of sacrifices before any work could be done in the fields at all.

When the weary ploughman plodded homeward, things were no better. Limentinus was installed on his threshold, Forculus had power over the door, with the fine distinction that if there were anything to do with the hinges, it was passed to Cardea for action.

To this were added, later, the high gods, borrowed from the Greeks, such as Jupiter, Mars, Neptune, Venus, and a hundred others. All had to be propitiated. Jupiter ruled the sky, Juno the air, Neptune the sea, Mercury ran business affairs, Minerva controlled men's thoughts, Liber and Libera presided over copulation, Venus over love-affairs and Mars over war.

The greater the god, the more particular he was over the form of his worship. No mistake was permitted, and we hear of occasions when a sacrifice had to be repeated as many as thirty times until it was right, the temple officials, naturally, being paid thirty times over.

It would scarcely seem possible that a religion more absurd could be invented, but it was done. What is more, it was added to the original creed and made obligatory. When an emperor died, the Senate met in solemn session and debated whether or not he had become a god. In the majority of cases, they decided that he had. It was then decreed that he should be worshipped and a temple was set up for the purpose.

The Senate, though servile, was not insane. The farce was not taken seriously. But the subsequent worship was taken very seriously indeed. Anybody refusing to sacrifice to an emperor's statue, even though that particular emperor had murdered the citizen's father, could be put to death.

But the worship of emperors, however preposterous, is profoundly interesting. By instituting it, the Romans contrived to prostitute the two finest ideas of Western civilisation, religious feeling and personal liberty. For nineteen hundred years Europe has fought to rid itself of this monstrosity. Down to this moment men are fighting, dying or languishing in prisons in an effort to prevent one powerful man dictating what they shall believe. The monuments of Rome are memorials of the source of the evil.

Why did the Romans do it? For the same reason that the French overthrew their constitution and put power in the hands of one man, Charles de Gaulle. We, in our times, can understand the process better than any of our predecessors. One section of the Roman populace threatened to become masters of the state. These were the newly-rich, whose wealth came from conquest. Having virtually unlimited money and no principles, they were able to suborn the rest. A rich man not only spent money in unparalleled sums for the purpose of getting himself or his candidates elected to office, he also attached to himself a host of parasites, known as his "clients", who ate at his table and did his bidding. Rome and its possessions threatened to be engulfed by a lewd-living, lawless, spendthrift and conspiratorial class of plutocrats. Julius Caesar, a man deep in the same corruption himself, found that by championing the people against the plutocrats, he could win what he most coveted, and that was power. It was thought that he, and he alone, could discipline Rome. Because of the glamour of his name, we assume that that is what he intended to do. But he was killed by Romans, who were convinced that he had no such intention. Caesar was struck down at the foot of Pompey's statue before he could demonstrate to history whether he was a great man or a great scoundrel. All that we can legitimately say of him is that he was a very able man. To what end, we do not know.

By the chances of civil war that followed his death, a young man of equal ability and less dubious aims emerged as Rome's master. He did not break the power of the plutocrats, but he counterbalanced it with his own. He did not reform the manners of the Romans, but he at least persuaded them that reform was desirable. He did not stop the destroying flood of wealth, but he diverted some of it to sound administration. Augustus was the equal of Julius Caesar in his ability to manage affairs, but he was free from the other's streak of the mountebank. He did not spend his spare time dreaming dreams of greatness. When he had finished with the day's business, his favourite pastime was to sit on the pavement and play dice with little boys. The Roman Senate, filled with patricians who were too sunk in frivolity, corruption or sheer idleness to govern, were eager to leave the job to him. Augustus, not without irony, gave it back to them. He governed, but in their name.

It was a deception. But men either govern themselves or they must be governed by tricks. Besides, Augustus was astute enough to appear, right to the end of a long life, to believe his own artifice. When he died, it seemed that the Romans had only to find a man like him to take over and they would have an ideal government. Not until Trajan, eighty-four years later, did they find him. By then, Augustus' pragmatical deception had landed Rome with the worship of emperors as semi-divine when they were alive, and wholly gods when they were dead.

The Senate, reluctant to govern, had discovered that it had no need to. It was willing to flatter anyone who would continue to save them the trouble. Among those that they flattered for this purpose were Caligula, Nero and Domitian. Such men, only half-human, found no difficulty in believing that they were half-divine. When a rough but sane soldier, Vespasian, won his way to the purple, he turned the matter off with a joke, but only on his deathbed ("I think," he said, "I am becoming a god."). By that time, the relationship of the Senate to the ruler had been fixed with satisfaction and profit to both sides.

Nor was the populace dissatisfied. It needed protection from the plutocrats, and in a way it got it. The Emperor became the greatest plutocrat of them all. As such he was able to terrorise the lesser men of wealth by murdering them, or confiscating their property, or both. Before the emperors, a man could become rich and risk nothing. Under them, he could still grow rich, but he risked his neck. As a system, it was rough and ready and sanguinary. But, after a fashion, it worked. So the Senate and the people were agreed that emperors should be told anything they liked to hear. There was, after all, no difficulty in calling a Caesar a god, even if one did not think much of him. The Romans did not think much of the gods either.

Besides, not all the emperors were incompetent. It was a great office, and as with other great positions in the world, men of large abilities sought it and sometimes won it. Others, already in the royal family by birth or adoption, were trained in their youth to their tremendous power, and, when they came to the purple, they did not disgrace it. Trajan, Hadrian and the Antonines, Diocletian and Constantine were gifted rulers of men. They despised (but they did not forego) the flattery. Some, such as Hadrian and Marcus Aurelius, made great efforts to justify it, and the people who lived under their rule were aware that they were remarkable men.

But it was absolute rule. Edward Gibbon considered that the time of the Antonines was the happiest in the history of man. Was it? Gibbon was a sober man in his judgments. But he began his book with the Antonines and he stood in need of a dramatic contrast to the decline that he traced through the succeeding volumes of his history: besides, he had little direct knowledge of living under a despotism. Nowadays we are better informed. Was life under rulers as powerful as Stalin really the climax of human happiness?

Like all absolute rulers, the "good" emperors, as they are known in

19 *An exceptionally well-carved sarcophagus found in Acilia in 1950. It is an example of the powerful influence of Greek things on the Roman mind. The figures here are Romans, but they are shown as Greek philosophers and poets. The sarcophagus has been tentatively dated as being made about 250 A.D.*

19

the history books, built lavishly. Classical Rome, as we see it today, is really their work. It is they who built the greater part of its surviving monuments. The work of the times before them and after has to be sought out and is unimpressive when it is found. The ruins of the "good" emperors' buildings dominate the heart of Rome.

I have spent many hours walking among them, and reconstructing the life that went on around them. Their size was stupendous. The column of Trajan now overshadows the ruins of his Forum. It looks as though it must have been the principal object there. In fact, the buildings of the Forum were so vast that the column was a mere ornament, equivalent, in proportion, to the figure-head of a wooden ship-of-the-line. The structures around it were covered with marble and heavily gilded, and astonished antiquity with their grandeur. It is still customary to marvel at these ruins and, at first, I did my share.

But, as the days that I spent among them lengthened into weeks and into whole seasons, I grew to know them, at least in plan, as well as the Romans who had seen them when they were new. I grew to feel small and oppressed. So did the Romans.

Gibbon was, vociferously, a gentleman and he spoke, I think, of gentlemen being happy in the age of the good emperors. He ignored the others, or was careless of their feelings. And, indeed, the life of a Roman gentleman in those times might have been happy enough, provided he held his tongue and the Emperor did not covet his fortune to pay for a new wing to one of his splendid buildings. But, for the others, we know it was frustrating and, above all, dull.

We have curious proof of this. The right of free association was denied to the Romans, as it is in Russia and China today. For any group of people to come together for any purpose in a regular manner, permission had to be obtained from the Palace. It was often denied, and always reluctantly given. The emperors regarded trade guilds with the greatest suspicion. They existed, because the Empire was too vast to be governed so minutely that they could be stopped. When they were discovered they were watched, and the first opportunity was taken to disband them. But association for some pious purpose was not so frowned upon, and the emperors were probably not unwilling that their subjects should spend their time thus instead of gossiping about politics. Since, officially, there were no politics except what went on inside the Emperor's head, any discussion of them was certainly lèse-majesté, and probably treason.

The populace, throttled back from all free expression, weighed down by an Imperial administration that punished criticism, saw their

20 *The Appian Way. It is lined with funerary monuments. The road was opened in 312 B.C. On the left is a circular tomb, on the right a 2nd-century sepulchral temple.*

21 *A sleeping Fury. The Romans adopted the Greek Erinyes, who were agents of vengeance. But it was a purely literary and artistic borrowing. There is no evidence that they were ever part of practised religion in Rome. In the National Museum of the Baths of Diocletian.*

49

loophole and made use of it. The Romans had only the vaguest notions of a life after death, and barely considered it when thinking about their end. But they had a great fear of being forgotten by the living. The humblest citizen had his tombstone, while the richest ones built elaborate tombs, some of which still stand along the Appian Way to remind the passer-by of the dead. Denied all other forms of association, the lower orders of society began to form funerary clubs. Someone would leave money in his will to endow a banquet that should be held annually to commemorate his death. It was attended by his relatives and friends, who drank to his memory. From this simple rite, the clubs expanded to a series of meetings. Excuses could be found, and none better than the commemoration of the dead and the Emperor's birthday, accession day, or marriage. As the clubs developed, they no longer depended on the dead man's bounty. Regular subscriptions were levied, funds were raised and disbursed in charitable works, sometimes to the dead man's children when they stood in need*.

In this gloomy manner, the lower classes of the Roman Empire satisfied that need of combining with one's fellows that the Imperial system otherwise forbade. As I shall show, this humble custom, transferred to another faith, shook the Empire to its foundations.

2

THE MOST FAMOUS COLLECTION OF ANTIQUITIES FROM IMPERIAL Rome is the Capitoline Museum. Let us suppose a Roman of, say, the time of the Flavian Emperors were to emerge from the chill shadows of Hades and re-visit his city. Suppose, too, like every other visitor he were to walk round the Capitoline Collection.

It is unlikely that he would find much to interest him in the major rooms. A statue or two might take his eye and revive a memory. But he would find few masterpieces. Most of what we treasure he would dismiss as journeyman copies made for gardens and secondary public buildings.

But one small room would move him profoundly, so deeply that he might well raise his hands and say a prayer. This small room is on the ground floor, half-open to the weather. It has about a dozen statues. Nothing in it is Roman, or even Greek. The statues are all Egyptian. There are large columns with reliefs of shaven-headed priests. There is a hawk, representing the Egyptian god Horus. There

22 *Trajan's Column, made of 18 blocks of marble, and, in all, 137 feet high and ornamented with 2500 carved figures, is the principal remaining monument of the Imperial Forum. The bas-reliefs around it tell the story of Trajan's expeditions. Until the year 1587, there was a statue of Trajan at the top of the column: in that year it was changed for one of St Peter. In the background is the church of St Mary of Loreto.*

* See Dill's *Roman Society from Nero to Marcus Aurelius* for a fuller treatment of this crucial subject than I can give here.

23 *The Roman Forum seen from the
Sacred Way. The arch in the middle
distance is that of the Emperor Septimus
Severus and the large building in the
background with the tower, on the
Capitoline Hill, is the present town-hall of
Rome.*

24 *Another view of the Roman Forum. In
the distance is the so-called Temple of
Romulus. It is believed to have been
constructed in the 4th century A.D. by the
joint-emperor Maxentius in honour of his
son, Romulus. It was later dedicated to
Constantine. In the 6th century, it became
part of the church of St Cosmas and
St Damian and it contains some 9th and
12th-century frescoes. In the foreground is
the house of the Vestals. There were six
Vestal priestesses and, amongst other duties,
they safeguarded valuable civic documents
and wills. After the triumph of Christianity, the house was lived in by imperial,
and subsequently by papal, officials.*

25 *The Mausoleum of Hadrian was started
in 139. It has a diameter of seventy yards.
Aurelian made a castle of it, and Theodoric
turned it into a prison. It remained both a
castle and a prison for many centuries and
has been reconstructed continually. Now it
is a museum of firearms. The bridge on the
left is the Ponte Sant'Angelo, which, until
recently, was the only bridge across
the Tiber that led conveniently to
St Peter's. This bridge was done over by
Gian-Lorenzo Bernini and the statues on it
were made according to his designs.*

is a red granite sphinx, two seated baboons, two lions, a crocodile, and another sphinx bearing the cartouche of the Pharaoh Amasis II.

All these were found a few hundred yards from my front door, under some narrow roads which I thread through every time I go to see the Forum. To a great number of Romans, the most sacred spot in their city was here, not in the Capitoline temple, not in the house of the Vestal Virgins and decidedly not in any of the temples erected to the Genius of Rome. It was in the Campus Martius, where rose the temple to the goddess Isis and the god Serapis, both deities from Egypt. The most revered men of religion would not be the official temple attendants endlessly repeating a ritual which long ago had lost any real meaning: reverence would be given to the men with shaven heads, some of whom had made themselves eunuchs the better to show their devotion to this goddess. Thus, the priests of Isis conducted the only religion in which a great many Romans really believed.

Today, the area is filled with churches, some of them cheek-by-jowl. Very often, when I have walked the narrow streets in the morning or in the early evening, I have gone inside the churches and seen lights, acolytes and priests in white. I have smelt incense from swinging thuribles, I have seen the glint of golden utensils, and I have heard singing.

It was just so, two thousand years ago. Isis and Serapis were worshipped each morning and each evening. There was a sacrifice in the morning and in the evening vespers were sung, as they are sung now on the days of the great feasts. Both ceremonies were of the greatest splendour, with a host of priests and attendants, with clouds of incense and singing to the sound of flutes and sistrums that had a strange and thrilling effect upon the listening Romans.

Everything was Egyptian and that was what the Romans liked about it. To go into the temple of Isis was to be able to escape for a while from the emptiness of life under the emperors. It meant worshipping a goddess, not a man. It meant offering money to priests who might in return give you a drink of water from a magic well, instead of to priests who would give you nothing at all except the assurance that you were a sound citizen. It meant running away for a little from the gilt and marble grandeur and this, to a Roman, became a need as deep as the need to breathe. Some, rich and noble, were able to escape to their villas in the countryside and by the sea. Others escaped to this foreign temple of a foreign faith.

It would seem that some of the emperors wanted to escape as well. Otho openly took part in the rites of Isis. Domitian, who once dodged assassination by disguising himself as one of her priests, rebuilt the temple in the Campus Martius and did it in the grand manner. Hadrian had statues of all the Egyptian gods in his villa and Commodus went so far as to shave his head in order to walk in a procession of the goddess.

It is impossible not to be curious about such a faith, but equally impossible to know anything exact about it. It is doubtful if many of its actual devotees knew precisely what their faith was. It was full of mystifications and secrets which were only partly revealed to the initiates. It is presumed that the high priests of the cult knew what these mysteries were, since they must have made them up. But, like so many of the really interesting parts of history, they have been lost to us. What little we do know does not suggest that the priests of Isis were men of any great moral elevation.

In the first place, the faith was firmly based on magic of the most puerile sort. It was thought that the goddess gave favoured initiates such fairy-tale powers as the ability to turn men into animals. The high-priests, naturally, had the power to turn them back again. Water from the Nile (or ostensibly from that river) was preserved in every temple, in a well. It was sold in little bottles and worked miracles of every sort, from healing the sick to rendering lovers invisible on awkward occasions.

Secondly, the heart of the mystery of the religion was as plain a piece of hocus-pocus as ever kept food in a priest's belly. Apuleius, who was an emotional convert to the faith, went through the major initiation ceremony. After telling us that he may not reveal what happened for fear of the goddess' displeasure, he goes on to give us a little glimpse. That done, he coyly remarks that we are none the wiser for what he has let slip. But that is not entirely true. We can make some deductions.

Apuleius narrates that, after being given a bath and sprinkled with holy water, he was put on a vegetarian, non-alcoholic, diet for ten days. At the end of that, surrounded by a flock of priests, he was dressed in white and taken to the inner sanctuary of the temple. There, he tells us, allusively, he approached "the gates of death and set one foot on the threshold." He was, however, permitted to remain alive, coming back to the land of the living by being drawn through "all the elements." It was now midnight, but the fortunate initiate "saw the sun shining as though it were high noon." He then saw the "gods of the underworld" quite close to, followed by "the gods of the skies." He worshipped them and emerged from the ordeal a re-born man. He tells us all this on the express condition that we believe it.

26 *This striking portrait in bronze is of Constantius, the son of the Emperor Constantine. It is considerably larger than life-size and can be seen in the Capitoline Museum.*

If we do not, some interesting facts emerge. Death has no threshold, the sun does not shine at midnight in Mediterranean latitudes, and there are no gods of either the underworld or the sky. But since he said he saw all these things, he must have seen something like them. In other words, he was subjected to a piece of theatrical hocus-pocus. A competent organiser of a modern amusement park would find little difficulty in arranging a tunnel-ride along similar lines, especially if his clients were religiously exalted and had been on short rations for a week or so. Apuleius unwittingly proves that whatever the central mystery of the religion of Isis was, it was not a spiritual exercise. It was a show. The Romans had a great passion for shows.

All this charlatanry was the best that the Roman Empire had to offer in the way of food for the soul, except for itinerant Greek professors of philosophy. But these brawled among themselves and were difficult to understand even when they intended that they should be understood, which was not always the case. It would not do, and it could not last. Plutarch tells us that Cassius, the conspirator against Julius Caesar, said to Brutus that he wished the gods existed because then he could believe in the justice of their cause. If he really said this, he showed himself to be one of the clearest-headed men in Rome. He had summed up the two things that were wrong with Rome and would remain wrong with Rome long after he was dead: tyranny, which he did his best to nip in the bud, and the lack of a moral code supported by some extra-human sanctions. He saw that without this no man can know whether he is doing right, or merely doing what it suits him to think is right.

3

As we all know, these unsatisfactory faiths were, in the end, replaced. Rome became Christian. My next expeditions in Rome were, therefore, to the tombs of St Peter and St Paul.

St Paul's tomb is buried under the piety and munificence of the ages. Nothing can be seen. St Peter's tomb—or rather where his tomb should be if there were one—is a different matter. It lies in a pagan cemetery in the foundations of his basilica. I could walk among the burial houses of the Romans, stir their bones with my finger and stand in the place where early Roman Christians believed St Peter had been interred after his execution.

I could not, however, do this without being accompanied by the Vatican guide. He was a well-trained man, and when we were gathered

27 *The Arch of Constantine was built in 315 A.D. in honour of Constantine's victory over Maxentius at the Milvian Bridge. The statues and friezes at the top, however, are from the 1st century. In the background, on the Palatine Hill, is the church of St Bonaventura.*

together on the burial place he told us, clearly and simply, the facts as they have been gathered from the Roman historians.

There had been a fire in Rome. Some suspected it had been started by the Emperor, who was Nero. Others were sure that it had been started by members of a new Jewish sect, the worshippers of Christ. The sect was persecuted, and St Peter died, crucified in the nearby circus.

I had known the story for many years. But it was not until I stood beneath St Peter's in that pagan cemetery that it occurred to me that there was something strange about it.

We have been taught that the early Christians were devout men and women who aimed at, and often succeeded in living, a pure, peaceful, gentle life consisting largely of prayer and good works. As they were so much nearer to the day when the Beatitudes were preached we imagine that these early Christians put them into practice more often than we do.

But why should such a mild lot of people be accused of deliberately setting fire to a whole city? Was it merely a calumny, or had they said something in public which would lead to the belief that they were capable of an act so catastrophic?

I made up my mind to go into the question. I found that they had.

Now, we have an excellent record of what these early Christians believed in the Acts and the Epistles. It is impossible to read these without feeling that here we have a genuine record of what they did and what they thought. It has been garbled; it has been touched up. But it is a record, not an invention.

We have an epistle from St Peter, which there is reason to suppose he actually wrote or, rather, dictated. At any rate, people, who knew him and heard him, felt it was sufficiently close to what he believed to go under his name.

He believed that the world was about to come to an end. "The end of all things is at hand," he advises his fellow-Christians. "... For the time is come that judgment must begin at the house of God." And it was not only a judgment day, it was "a glory that shall be revealed." He is quite clear that this will happen soon. "The last days" is his phrase for the years in which he lived.

St Paul did not always see eye to eye with St Peter. They had, as we know, a stand-up quarrel. But in this matter they were quite in agreement. In writing to the Thessalonians, he encourages them by saying that those who are giving them trouble will be troubled by God in

28 *These two frescoes, which can be seen in the Oratory of St Sylvester in the church of SS. Quattro Coronati, demonstrate the relationship between the Pope and the Emperor, from the point of view of the popes. They were painted in the 13th century. In the picture on the left, the Pope is receiving a crown from the Emperor Constantine. In the second, the Emperor is showing his submission to the will of the Pope by his formal holding of the Pope's horse's head whilst he, in his turn, wears his imperial crown. This is a prime example of ecclesiastical wishful-thinking and hind-sight, since nothing of the sort occurred. Constantine permitted the practice of the Christian faith, but he submitted to no pope.*

29 *This Roman mosaic floor was found, during recent excavations, under the Basilica of St John Lateran.*

28

29

31

32

return, while they, the Christians, "will rest with us, when the Lord Jesus shall be revealed from heaven with his mighty angels, in flaming fire, taking vengeance on them that know not God . . . when He shall come to be glorified in his saints, and to be admired in all them that believe in that day."

What exactly was "that day," the final one in these "last days"? The question was most specifically answered by Jesus himself in words which are perfectly clear in their meaning. It is put down in the Gospel of St Matthew, one of the four records of what the Christians could remember of the teachings of the Founder.

Jesus and the disciples had been talking of the Temple of Jerusalem and Jesus had told them that it will be destroyed. Jesus, then, went to the Mount of Olives and "the disciples came unto him privately, saying, 'Tell us, when shall these things be? And what shall be the sign of the coming, and of the end of the world?'

"And Jesus answered and said unto them, 'Take heed that no man deceive you.

'For many shall come in my name, saying, "I am the Christ"; and shall deceive many.

'And ye shall hear of wars and rumours of wars: see that ye be not troubled: for all these things must come to pass, but the end is not yet.

'For nation shall rise against nation, and kingdom against kingdom: and there shall be famines, and pestilences, and earthquakes, in divers places.

'All these are the beginning of sorrows.

'Then shall they deliver you up to be afflicted, and shall kill you: and ye shall be hated of all nations for my name's sake.

'And then shall many be offended, and shall betray one another, and shall hate one another.

'And many false prophets shall rise, and shall deceive many.

'And because iniquity shall abound, the love of many shall wax cold.

'But he that shall endure unto the end, the same shall be saved.

'And this gospel of the kingdom shall be preached in all the world for a witness unto all nations, and then shall the end come.

'When ye therefore shall see the abomination of desolation, spoken of by Daniel the prophet, stand in the holy place (whoso readeth, let him understand).

'Then let them which be in Judaea flee into the mountains:

'Let him which is on the housetop not come down to take any thing out of his house:

30 *A fresco of the old Basilica of St John Lateran. It was founded by Pope Melchiades in 311 A.D. as the cathedral of Rome, and dedicated to the Redeemer. Destroyed in part by the Vandals, it was restored by St Leo the Great in the 5th-century. It was wrecked by an earthquake in 896, and rebuilt by Popes Sergius III and Nicolas IV. Laid waste a third time in 1361, it was reconstructed during the pontificates of Urban V and Gregory XI. Finally, the great architect Borromini completely redecorated the church for the Jubilee of 1650 during the pontificate of Innocent X.*

31, 32 *These photographs show models of the Lateran Palace as it was in medieval times. It was the official residence of the popes until they left Rome for Avignon. It was burned down, along with the basilica, in 1308 and never rebuilt. For this reason the popes, on their return from Avignon, settled in the Vatican.*

33 *A ceiling mosaic in the church of St Costanza. On the left of the picture there is a scene of wine-pressing. The church was built as a mausoleum for the daughters of Constantine: it soon after became a baptistery and in 1254 a church. This mosaic is among the very earliest known Christian mosaics: the head in the centre is believed to represent Costanza's husband.*

'Neither let him which is in the field return back to take his clothes.

'And woe unto them that are with child, and to them that give such in those days!

'But pray ye that your flight be not in the winter, neither on the sabbath day:

'For then shall be great tribulation, such as was not since the beginning of the world to this time, no, nor ever shall be. . .

'Behold I have told you before.

'Wherefore if they shall say unto you, "Behold he is in the desert"; go not forth: "Behold he is in the secret chambers"; believe it not.

'For as the lightning cometh out of the east and shinest even unto the west; so shall also the coming of the Son of man be.

'For wheresoever the carcase is, there will be the eagles gathered together.

'Immediately after the tribulation of those days shall the sun be darkened, and the moon shall not give her light, and the stars shall fall from heaven, and the powers of the heavens shall be shaken:

'And then shall appear the sign of the Son of man in heaven: then shall all the tribes of the earth mourn, and they shall see the Son of man coming in the clouds of heaven with power and great glory.

'And he shall send his angels with a great sound of a trumpet, and they shall gather together his elect, from the four winds, from one end of heaven to the other.

'Now learn a parable of the fig tree; When his branch is yet tender, and putteth forth leaves, ye know that summer is nigh:

'So likewise ye, when ye shall see all these things, know that it is near, even at the doors.

'Verily, I say unto you, This generation shall not pass, till all these things be fulfilled.'"

The meaning of the words is plain. But the generation that heard them did pass, and the world survived. So did the next and the next. The world, as we know, is still with us. But, for these early generations, so tremendous a prophecy coming from so sublime a source changed their whole way of thinking. They believed that Rome and every other place on earth would be destroyed by fire in their own lifetimes. They must have said so, from the rooftops, because if they said anything about their faith at all (and they were zealous propagandists), they could scarcely have omitted so startling a part of it.

Then, as it happened, in A.D. 64 a disastrous and unexplained fire did burn Rome. What could be more natural than to assume that it had been started by an irresponsible sect of fanatics who were careless

34, 35 These bas-reliefs are from a 3rd-century Christian sarcophagus. The first represents Jonah and the Whale, and the other, the Good Shepherd and the Baptism of Jesus. They can be seen in the church of Santa Maria Antiqua, one of the oldest churches in Rome.

36 Immediately below the crypt of St Peter's is an ancient pagan Roman cemetery. A large number of sepulchral rooms or "houses" have been excavated and most resemble the one in this picture. They all have niches, frescoed walls, stucco-work, funerary urns and inscriptions on the floor. It is amongst these tombs that St Peter is believed to have been buried.

34

35

37

38

39

37 *There are over twenty catacombs in Rome where the early Christians met, buried their martyrs and celebrated their simple rites. This wall-painting of Christ and the Apostles can be seen in the catacomb of St Domitilla. It is considered to be either late 3rd century or early 4th.*

38 *In the cemetery of St Priscilla, on the Via Salaria, is this painting of Shadrach, Meshach and Abednego in the fiery furnace. First half of the 4th century.*

39 *In the catacomb known from the 3rd century as St Callixtus', which was the official cemetery of the bishops of Rome, is this painting which shows Moses striking the rock out of which water gushed. End of the 4th century.*

40 *There are thirty-six mosaics on the walls of the central nave of St Mary Major, which narrate Old Testament episodes from the lives of Abraham, Isaac, Moses and Joshua. They were made not later than the first half of the 5th century. It is considered possible, however, that they were transferred from the original basilica of Pope Liberius, in which case the mosaics would be from the 4th century. The lower panel here, for example, shows Moses, with Caleb and Joshua, son of Nun, in the desert, being stoned by the Jews after he had brought the bad news about there being powerful inhabitants in Canaan, the promised land, in which the Jews had hoped to settle peacefully. The top panel shows the return of those whom Moses and Aaron had sent to spy out the land.*

of their actions since they believed all was coming to an end very shortly? What could be more natural than to decide that, inebriated with apocalyptic dreams, they had advanced the date of the Last Judgment by trying to start it up on their own?

The fact that the world did not come to an end was a puzzle to all good Christians, and it still is, although all but theologians continue to ignore it. It is known as the eschatological problem and, for those who can bear with theological writing, it has given rise to some of the most interesting books in Christian literature*. They are worthy of study, because the eschatological teachings of Jesus were at the root of the Christian view: and they were the main reason why Christianity swept aside the pagan faith and the mystery religions, finally to conquer the Roman Empire.

Let us consider these early Christians (and I speak especially of those who were Romans). Let us see more clearly what they were really like.

In the first place they had no morals. They had abandoned their own pagan faith which, in any case, did not supply them with any precise moral rules. They no longer respected the Emperor, to whom they were rude, calling him such things as the Abomination of Desolation and other epithets from the extensive vocabulary of the Jewish prophets. They were in the happy state of having been saved from the wrath which was shortly coming, and had nothing to do but wait.

St Paul, however, had other ideas. He was a very busy man, and like other busy people he had no use for people who had no morals. He was aware that unless his converts obeyed some rules, he would never know what they were up to when his back was turned. His letters to the early churches are clear evidence that he had judged the situation rightly. While they contain transcendent wisdom, they also contain a good deal of downright abuse. In St Paul's time, it would seem that Christians were called upon to obey almost no ritual save praying and having a meal together. They could not, it appears, do even that in a seemly manner, some of them gobbling up the provisions they had brought with them with indecent haste, besides showing other and worse signs of licence.

He set about building a moral structure for the new faith to keep the converts in order until the day of reckoning. We, in the Christian world, live inside that structure to this day. That was a remarkable feat, even supposing that much has been written into his texts. And, in truth,

* For example, *The Background of the New Testament and its Eschatology*, which are studies by a group of international scholars, published in honour of C. H. Dodd and edited by W. D. Davies and D. Daube.

71

St Paul was a remarkable man. He had a most original point of view. Nowadays, we all share it, if we are civilised, even when we are not Christians. St Paul put his hope in the future.

It is difficult for us, today, to realise what a profound revolution in thinking that was. Perhaps it is only in Rome, where one can turn in a moment from the monuments of the pagans to those of Christianity, that one can really come to understand the change. The men who walked in the vast marble forums, or sat in the tiers of the enormous amphitheatres, or lived in the grossest luxury in their villas, looked back to the past as the Golden Age. We have seen the myth that they made out of it. They thought about the present as we all do: when they were in luck, they liked it, when they were out, they cursed it. But of the future they did not think at all. Rome was to them really an eternal city. When in it, you did as the Romans did, because that was the way a sensible man behaved and always would do. There was good and bad in the Roman way of life, they knew. But they did not look forward to the good increasing and the bad being stamped out. A few men with a philosophical turn of mind might try to improve themselves, but not one of them ever imagined that the brute mass of citizenry could be cajoled or forced into following their example. They would have considered any such suggestion as offensive.

The Romans had no idea of progress. Emperors might have thought of buildings getting vaster and roads getting longer, but not much. The buildings soon grew to be as big as anybody needed, and as the Empire adjusted its boundaries, roads were shortened rather than extended. If any Roman ever thought of a world where people could lead happier lives, he must have thought in terms of more shows in the amphitheatre. But these already took up a large part of the year. Imperial Rome was a static society, enlivened, but not changed, by occasionally throwing murdered emperors into the gutters.

The Christians reversed all this. To them, it did not matter a jot how fine and frugal the early Romans had been. There was no Golden Age in the past that could compare with the glory and peace that was to come. The pagan Roman made much of his long ancestry, if he had one. The Christians thought nothing at all of family trees. The Tree on which Christ died towered immeasurably above all of them. If the past had any meaning or importance, it would only be discovered after the Second Coming. This was the key to all things, the end of all things, and the beginning of real living. The Book of the Revelation of St John which, to so many Christians nowadays, seems to be tacked on to the end of the New Testament read very differently in those

41 *The interior of the church of St Sabina on the Aventine Hill. It was founded in the 5th century and went through several transformations until in 1936 the Dominican Order, to whom the church belongs, had it restored to what it was thought the church looked like at some time during the Middle Ages.*

43

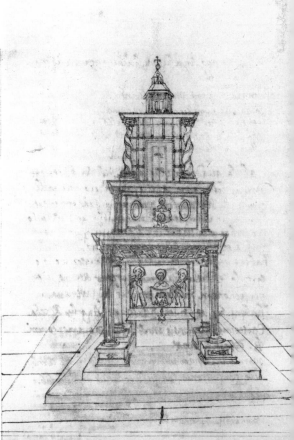

44

Exemplum Ciborij marmorei in sacello Joann
Septimi in veteri Vaticana Basilica ad contin
dum Sacrosanctũ Sudariũ Veronicæ à dicto S
mo Pontifice exstructi.

42 *The interior of the basilica of St Clement. The original church of St Clement was built in 385. It was destroyed by the Norman, Robert Guiscard, in 1084. In 1108, this second church was built on top of the one destroyed. In the centre of the church is the choir, surrounded by a wall of cosmatesque marble. On the right is a pulpit. The original 4th-century church was discovered about a hundred years ago under this church, when a small temple, dedicated to the pagan god Mithra, was also unearthed in the foundations. Thus there are three places of worship to be seen, one on top of the other.*

43 *The purpose of this elegant 13th-century ambry was to safeguard sacramental vessels. It is in cosmatesque style and can be seen in the church of St Clement (see Plate 42).*

44 *This is a drawing of a reliquary which, in the 8th century, was in St Peter's. It was lost when St Peter's was rebuilt. This record of it, from a manuscript in the Vatican Library, shows that the reliquary once held the Veil of St Veronica, upon which the face of Jesus was said to be printed. The veil is now kept in a room in one of the central piers of St Peter's, above the statue of St Veronica. It is exhibited, very briefly, once a year, but at a distance from the congregation that makes it impossible to distinguish the detail.*

45 *Another view of the restored St Sabina. See Plate 41.*

early days. To the first Christians, it was the essential final chapter to the story of the birth, ministry, death and resurrection of the Founder of their faith. History was done with. The present was a time of waiting. Everything that could possibly interest a man or a woman or a child was in the future.

But time passed, and did not stop. There was no Second Coming. The wait continued from father to son, to his son's son, till the first who had waited were themselves part of a history that they thought had finished. Expectancy became hope, hope became faith, and, faith enduring, gave rise to commonsense. Second Coming or no, it was seen that the Christians were right. The only way to live bearably in the world of Rome was to believe that there was something better to come in heaven or on earth. There was the terrestrial city, with its temples, its marbles, its emperors, and its gold. But there was also a City of God where the pure of heart could live undefiled and the sinner be cleansed. It was, at last, seen to be nonsense to think that Rome was the summit of men's desires and their capacities. Men were baptised and breathed freely again. They had hope in the midst of suffocating abundance.

The success of Christianity in Rome was certain. It supplied the thing which Romans most lacked. They were conscious that they were a great people, the greatest people in the known world. But they lacked a moral purpose. They could get richer and more powerful. They could conquer more and more territory. But the world was small and conquests as they spread wider grew more and more unprofitable. There was little point in being master of semi-naked barbarians. Rome could civilise, but no Roman could feel that as his mission. His own civilisation had been wholly borrowed. He was anxious to borrow more rather than to act as a school-teacher.

Then Christianity came with its message that empire and culture, the arts of war and the arts of peace were flimsy, evanescent and of no importance to a serious man. The moral purpose of a man was to live a life acceptable to the Lord, who would one day come in glory. St Paul had shown him how such a life should be led, and there were, in addition, the sublimities of the teachings of Christ. A sensible man had nothing to do but try his best to live accordingly. That would take him every minute of his life and every ounce of his energy. Life had a meaning.

A Christian Roman was no longer at the mercy of an emperor's whims. He was still under a dictatorship, but it was a divine one. The Emperor's wishes were only those of a mortal man. It was wise to obey them if one could (St Paul had said so, and so had Jesus). But if it could not be done without harm to one's true, immortal life, then it need not be done. A Roman who became a Christian was, at once, removed from the phantasmagoric world of living under the absolute rule of one man, and passed into the real world where a man was responsible for his own actions. He changed from knowing what was politic, to knowing what was good. He knew that wrong was permanently so, and did not change with dynasties. A Roman Christian was free.

4

FREE PEOPLE IN A DESPOTISM FREQUENTLY GET THEMSELVES KILLED as public nuisances. This happened to the Christians. The first cause of the triumph of Christianity was that it made sense. The second was that it had martyrs. I shall now examine how this was so.

The first martyrs of the Christian faith are held in great reverence. Some of their names are mentioned in the most solemn passages of the Mass. This reverence is due to them, because the faith was founded on their blood. But this fact, which they would not possibly have known, has coloured our view of them.

We have been taught to think of them as good men and women going to a terrible death to set an example of steadfastness to their fellows, and to strengthen the young Church. We admire their heroism. We marvel at their self-abnegation.

It is probable that they would have found our attitude toward them highly irritating. They had no intention of cementing the Church with their blood. There was no Church to cement. There were only groups of believers, who, like the martyrs, were convinced that the world was coming to an end. Therefore, a martyr entering the arena and facing the spectators could afford to feel smug. *They* were killing him. But he knew full well that in a very short time, *he* would be alive and they would be dead.

It was this superior attitude on the part of the martyrs that enraged the populace against them. Nowadays, if we see a man with a placard saying "The End of the World is at Hand," we pity him. But the first time that this extraordinary doctrine was publicly preached, it was thought so inhuman as to be bestial. Its promulgators were stitched into the skins of wild animals and thrown to dogs to be torn to pieces "not so much," remarks the historian, Tacitus, "on the charge of arson as for hatred of the human race." The accusation of setting fire to the city had flushed the Christians out. When Rome saw what she had in

46 *The chapel of St Zeno in the church of St Prassede is famous for its glowing mosaics, done in the Byzantine style. Both the church and the mosaics are from the 9th century.*

47 *This Madonna and Child, also from the same chapel of the same church of St Prassede, is one of the most important Byzantine mosaics in Rome.*

the midst of her ("Rome," as Tacitus says in the same passage, "that receptacle for everything that is sordid and degrading from every quarter of the globe"), the Roman populace set about stamping it to death.

It is hard for us to escape the mental picture of these men and women as clear-eyed, innocent, clad in white and going to their death with linked hands, singing hymns. The Romans accused them of such crimes as cannibalism, infanticide and incest. It is difficult to believe that, had they been as prepossessing a group as we could wish, such charges would have stuck. To the Romans, the early Christians appeared as infuriated maniacs with an unholy thirst for violence that could only be quenched by the blood of the whole human race. This attitude toward them lasted a long time. Tertullian, writing in A.D. 197, reveals this very clearly, when he asks why, if the Christians are criminals, they are treated worse than their fellow-criminals. Why, he demands, are they not allowed even to plead for themselves? "Because," he says, "that alone is looked for, which the public hate requires—the confession of the Name, not the investigation of the charge."

So much for the pagan view of the martyrs. Provided that we remember that they were not propagating the Sermon on the Mount but the terrors of the Apocalypse, we cannot feel it was wholly unreasonable.

What did surviving Christians think of them? In the first place, they thought the martyrs very lucky people. In only a little time, all Christians would get their reward—these for certain, because they had no risk of backsliding. Secondly, they thought that the martyrs were witnesses to the faith, not as we would regard a missionary slain by savages, but as something much more direct. Christ had conquered death. These were not dead, but sleeping. They willingly allowed themselves to be killed because, painful as it might be for a while, it really did not matter.

Their bodies, then, were joyfully collected whenever they could be found, and buried, not too deep, to await the final day. In some cases, the sarcophagus was placed in a niche, in the Roman fashion. In that case, it became the custom to celebrate the ritual meal upon the lid. To this day, in every Catholic altar, there is a small receptacle in which are placed the remains of a saint or a martyr, to which the priest, in saying Mass, refers directly. He echoes the voices of his earliest forerunners.

Let us look back for a moment at the Roman world, as we have

48, 49 *The imminence of the end of the world and the last judgment was, for centuries, an essential and dramatic part of Christian teaching. Michelangelo's Last Judgement in the Sistine Chapel is probably the best-known pictorial representation of it. This fresco, by the Roman painter, Pietro Cavallini, in the Convent of Santa Cecilia is a more tranquil rendering. It was painted in 1293 and shows Jesus, the Madonna, John the Baptist, apostles and angels. The detail in Plate 48 shows two of the apostles and that in Plate 49 is of two angels.*

seen it. It was ruled by emperors who were worshipped as divine. Their power was absolute. To protect it they forbade men meeting together. Nevertheless, as I have said, men did meet under the strange guise of burial societies.

Now the Christians were a secret society. We have a letter from Pliny the Younger in which he specifically points this out to the Emperor Trajan. Speaking of the sect in Bithynia, he says that after a ceremony "it was their custom to depart and meet again to take food; but it was ordinary and harmless food, and they ceased this practice after my edict in which, in accordance with your orders, I had forbidden secret societies."

They ceased the practice in Bithynia. But they did not in Rome. Instead, as we would expect, they set up a sort of burial society, meeting together to celebrate the anniversaries of the birth of the martyrs which, as was logical, was the day of their martyrdom. The vast, gloomy and intricate caverns of Rome, which are known as the Catacombs, were the place of their meeting.

Here, in due course, they gathered enough numbers and confidence to defy the emperors and to refuse to sacrifice to their statues. This unparalleled impertinence brought them a flock of new martyrs and, for the reason we have seen, a host of converts. In the end, they emerged from the Catacombs to convert the Emperor himself. Classical Rome was dead.

PART THREE   *Popes, kings and fairy-tales*

1

As we know from the history of our own times, one of the arts of governing men is to tell them a successful lie, and the bigger the better. I shall now describe one of the most successful untruths in the whole story of Western civilisation. It was concocted by ecclesiastics, but it is worthy of Sinbad the Sailor. Popes and kings believed it: bloody wars were fought for it; and nobody, for centuries, stopped to ask if it were true.

We have seen that when St Peter died he and his followers believed that the Second Coming was upon them. But the centuries passed, and there was no visible sign of Christ upon earth, except the Church. But which Church? There were a great number of them. There were powerful bishops obeyed by hundreds of thousands of the faithful in such places as Antioch, Constantinople, Alexandria and Rome. They often quarrelled between themselves. When they did, who was to decide which one of them was right? If the Church was the only sign of Christ that the world had, it should not speak with two voices. It must speak, loudly and clearly, with one. Whose?

The bishops of Rome said it should be theirs. They immediately, thereby, outraged the bishops of all the other great Sees. One argument of the Romans was that their Church had been founded by two apostles. The others had been founded by one. But this arithmetical quibble was soon dismissed by the other bishops as frivolous. Rome needed a better argument and there was one to hand.

Round the dome of St Peter's, circling the tomb of the Apostle and the altar, where the Pope says Mass, is a legend in golden letters. It repeats the verses from the Bible in which Jesus said to the Prince of the Apostles:

"Thou art Peter and upon this rock I will build my church; and the gates of hell shall not prevail against it. And I will give unto thee the keys of the Kingdom of Heaven."

The letters of this quotation are five feet high. They are backed up by innumerable representations of armorial bearings of the popes, which always include two crossed keys. I had observed it some twenty times when it occurred to me to find out what it really meant. I laboured among the works of the early Fathers of the Church (to whom all go for enlightenment in matters of faith) and here, briefly, is what I found.

Tertullian said the "rock" was St Peter. Origen disagreed and said that the "rock was every faithful follower of Our Lord." Augustine said the "rock" was St Peter but the power of the keys was given to all twelve Apostles. Tertullian said it was not. Cyprian said the power descended to all bishops: Origen said it descended only to good ones. Anselm split the powers of the keys into two: Gregory VII agreed with him, but Cyril of Alexandria disagreed with both, because he maintained that St Peter will receive the keys only after the Resurrection. Cyprian disagreed with himself: in some manuscripts he says that, on the contrary, it was founded on all the Apostles. Irenaeus says it was founded on St Peter *and* St Paul.

I could go on, but I doubt if the reader would stay with me. Let it suffice to say that the controversy raged for a long time, sometimes in the form of the subtlest theological disputation, sometimes in the form of bishops trying to settle it with a bout of fisticuffs amongst themselves. Councils of the Church were held to settle this (and allied matters), at which monks stood ready with staves to break the heads of their opponents should the Holy Ghost take the opposing side. But if the whole Christian world refused to acknowledge the Pope as its head (and it still so refuses) the prestige of the popes grew steadily, especially among the illiterate barbarians to the north and west of Italy, where the popes had sent missionaries, who converted whole nations. It has grown with a few setbacks, down to this day, when the bishop of Rome, as the successor of St Peter, is the spiritual head of one fifth of the human race.

I went to see him.

2

I SAW, IN FACT, TWO POPES, AND I SAW THEM MANY TIMES. I SAW them on so many occasions that I got to know them as well as a cathedral-goer knows his own, and lesser, bishop. For I realised that to see the Pope once or twice in a lifetime is to be overwhelmed by the transcending greatness of the office and the devotion, in these days, of the man who holds it. This had been my own experience as a pilgrim. But now my pilgrimages in Rome had a different purpose. I had seen with the eyes of faith. I now wished to observe with my own.

50 *This medieval scroll shows a cleric reading the Exultet during the Easter Ceremonies. The men in the foreground are making a procession in the church, perhaps to light the Paschal Candle. It is interesting to note that the writing at the top and bottom of this picture is upside-down. In this way, the scroll served a double purpose: the cleric could read it, and the congregation could look at the pictures as the scroll unfolded in the manner shown.*

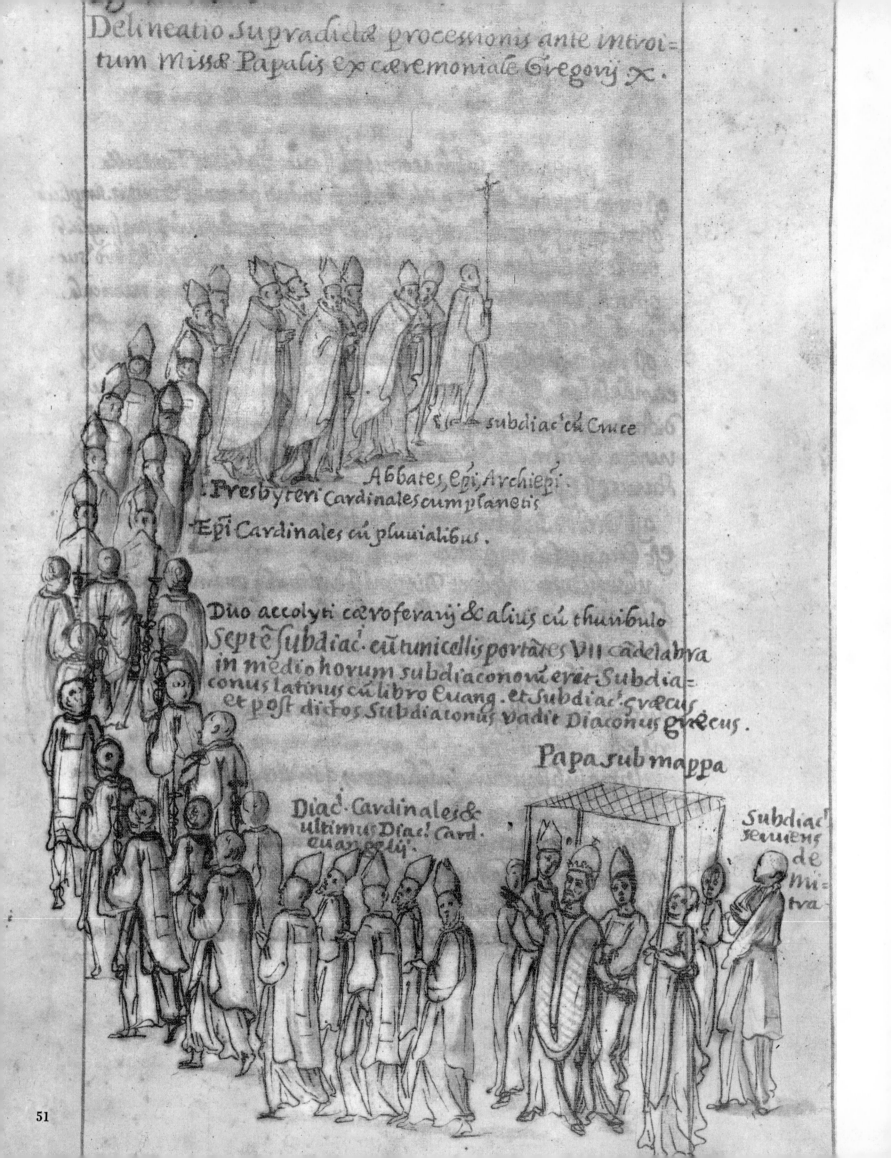

Delineatio supradictæ processionis ante introi-
tum Missæ Papalis ex cæremoniale Gregorij X.

subdiac̄ cū Cruce

Abbates, Epi, Archiepi.
Presbyteri Cardinales cum planetis

Epi Cardinales cū pluuialibus.

Duo accolyti cærofcrarij & alius cū thuribulo
Septē subdiac̄. cū tunicellis portātes VII cādelabra
in medio horum subdiaconorū erit Subdiaconus latinus cū libro Euang. et Subdiac̄ græcus
et post dictos Subdiaconus vadit Diaconus græcus.

Papa sub mappa

Diac̄. Cardinales &
ultimus Diac̄. Card.
Euangelij.

Subdiac̄
seruiens
de
Mi-
tra

51

UT SV
PER
BENE
DIC
TIO
NIS
MVN
S AC
COM
MO
DES

52

SCS
PE
TR
VS

+ SCISSIMVS
DN
LE
O
PP

D.N.
+ :: CARVLO

REX

DONAS
BICTO
A

As all the world knows, a pope makes his public appearances on a portable throne, surrounded by guards in picturesque uniforms, and followed by ecclesiastics of various grades. There are also around him a number of functionaries, who usually attract little attention. But after I had clapped and cheered the pontiff on several occasions, they attracted mine. I noticed that they had the bearing of aristocrats with the expressions of flunkeys, and I had seen the combination before.

Twenty or more years ago, I had spent some time as the guest of ruling princes. This was in India, but all over the world courtiers are alike. They all suffer, with dignity, a tyrannous employer. It does not matter how benevolent a ruler may be towards his subjects, how constitutionally modest in his actions, to his courtiers, he is a pitiless dictator. This must be so, however much the prince may wish it otherwise. A ruler maintains his position by the effect he creates upon his subjects. His courtiers are his stage-managers, his stage-hands, and his chorus. He cannot afford to let them make mistakes.

Now the Pope wears a triple crown. He wears splendid jewels and gleaming mantles. He sits upon a throne and cardinals do him obeisance. All this was familiar to me, as it is to everybody else. I had always discounted it as being done to the greater glory of the Church. I did not consider it an essential part of the papacy. We could have popes (I thought) without it, just as we can have ceremonies at an altar without the utensils being necessarily of gold. The Pope, I knew, ruled the faithful (and his tiny state of the Vatican City) but I did not consider that he needed his regal trappings to do it. After all, I had seen and I had met viceroys and, although they tried, they by no means equalled the Pope in the matter of worldly pomp.

But here were the unmistakable courtiers. So here, too must be a Court. A Court must surround a prince. It therefore followed that the successor of the Prince of the Apostles must be a prince in a very different and much more earthly sense.

I frequented the Court, a thing I was able to do because I was writing about the Vatican. I watched the procedure of Papal Audiences. They are far from religious ceremonies. There are chamberlains, attendants in knee-breeches, gentlemen-at-arms, a noble guard and soldiers, albeit private to the Pope, everywhere. One is led through apartment after apartment guarded by men-at-arms, who, with a telling sense of drama, rise in rank the nearer one gets to the pontiff. There is a damask-hung room with a throne, in which men of the highest rank in the Court stand about in little waiting groups, as I had seen them do so many times before in tropical throne-rooms. Then there is a flurry, a

51 *13th-century protocol for a papal procession in a drawing of a fresco that once existed in St John Lateran. The drawing is in the Vatican Library. The ceremony shown here is of the Pope, in full regalia and crown, taking possession of his See at St John Lateran.*

52 *The lighting of the Paschal Candle. This is done whilst the figure on the left reads the Exultet and a symbolical gesture of peace is shown from heaven. The picture is from a miniature in a 10th-century Exultet Roll in the Vatican Library.*

53 *Here St Peter is represented dividing spiritual and temporal power between Pope Leo III and the Emperor Charlemagne. Ecclesiastical power is symbolised by the pallium, and imperial power by a banner. The original mosaic of this was made in the 9th century, whilst both Leo and Charlemagne were alive. This picture is a 17th-century copy in water-colour, in the Vatican Library, of all that then remained of the original design.*

stiffening to attention and the Pope walks in preceded by his chief chamberlain who, without actually walking backwards, contrives to look as though he is doing so. The pontiff himself—and this is the rule whoever he may be—is affable and relaxed. He speaks to his visitors, each briefly: and, following the protocol of courts everywhere, he never says anything particularly striking. However, what he says is spoken, it would seem, directly and personally to the visitor he is greeting—an art mastered by kings, queens and princes all the world over. There is also that touch of idiosyncracy which makes all Courts, ridden by formality, still capable of providing an unexpected experience. The whim of the monarch is all. A person who has spent a life in devotion and good works will kneel to the Pope, kiss his ring and be given a few simple words of praise and encouragement. They are no doubt a memory he or she will treasure for a lifetime. But next to him may be a man who is introduced to His Holiness as (to invent an example) the manufacturer of a car the Pope is thinking of buying. He does not kneel, because he is not a Catholic. He does not kiss the Pope's ring, because the pontiff adroitly takes his hand in a normal handshake to avoid embarrassing him. But he will have five minutes' lively conversation with the Head of the Church who, like all royalty, will amaze him with his knowledge of the technical details of his profession.

It is true that the ceremony ends on a different note. But both the popes that I have been privileged to wait upon are so aware of this that they themselves change the tone. The Pope takes his place on the steps of the throne, lowers his voice and with great benignity invites his audience to receive the Apostolic Blessing. This solemn and moving moment over, the Pope goes quickly away and his visitors are once more ushered through the series of apartments attended, this time, by guards in descending order of rank. Apart from the Blessing, it has all been very worldly.

There are many other resemblances to other courts that I observed. The Vatican is a gossippy place, the best gossip being rapidly relayed from the courtier who has been nearest to and longest with the Sovereign Pontiff that morning. The Pope's displeasure is a disaster. An angry pope—and popes are not always benign—casts the Court into a gloom that may last until lunch-time. A happy pope, briskly going through his appointments and polishing off a couple of cardinals in under protocol time, makes everybody happy. There are smiles all round and, in the most relaxed way, minor officials take a little time off to smoke in those secret places where smoking may be unobserved if not actually permitted.

54 *St Peter's, where Charlemagne was crowned, looked like this in medieval times. This first basilica was built between 324 and 349 A.D. above the tomb of St Peter on Vatican Hill and it is customarily referred to as Constantine's basilica. It was torn down by Pope Julius II, and the present edifice was started on Bramante's designs in 1506. In the foreground is an enormous bronze pine-cone, which probably was on the top of Hadrian's mausoleum in Roman times. It is now in the Cortile della Pigna, one of the courtyards of the Vatican Palace. The artist placed it inside the church for the sake of his picture, but actually it was always in the atrium. See Plate 93.*

55

56

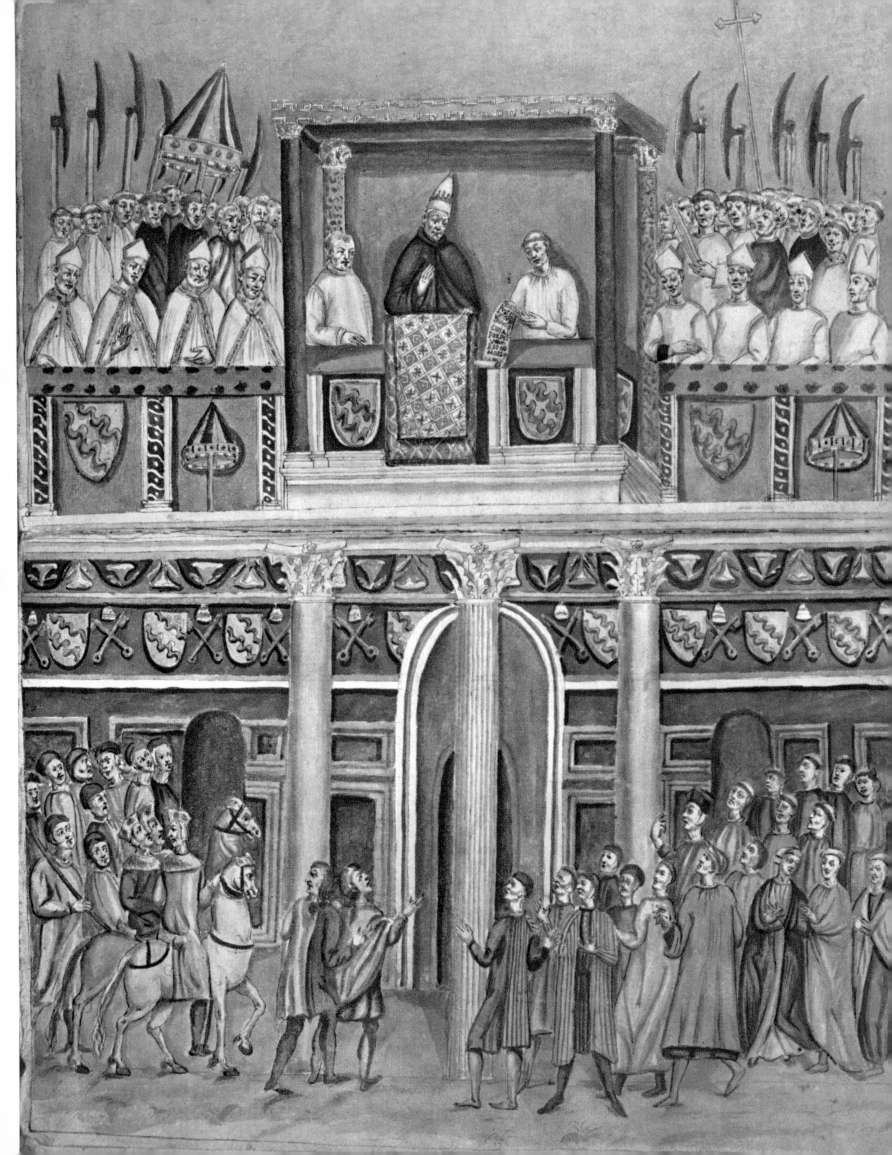

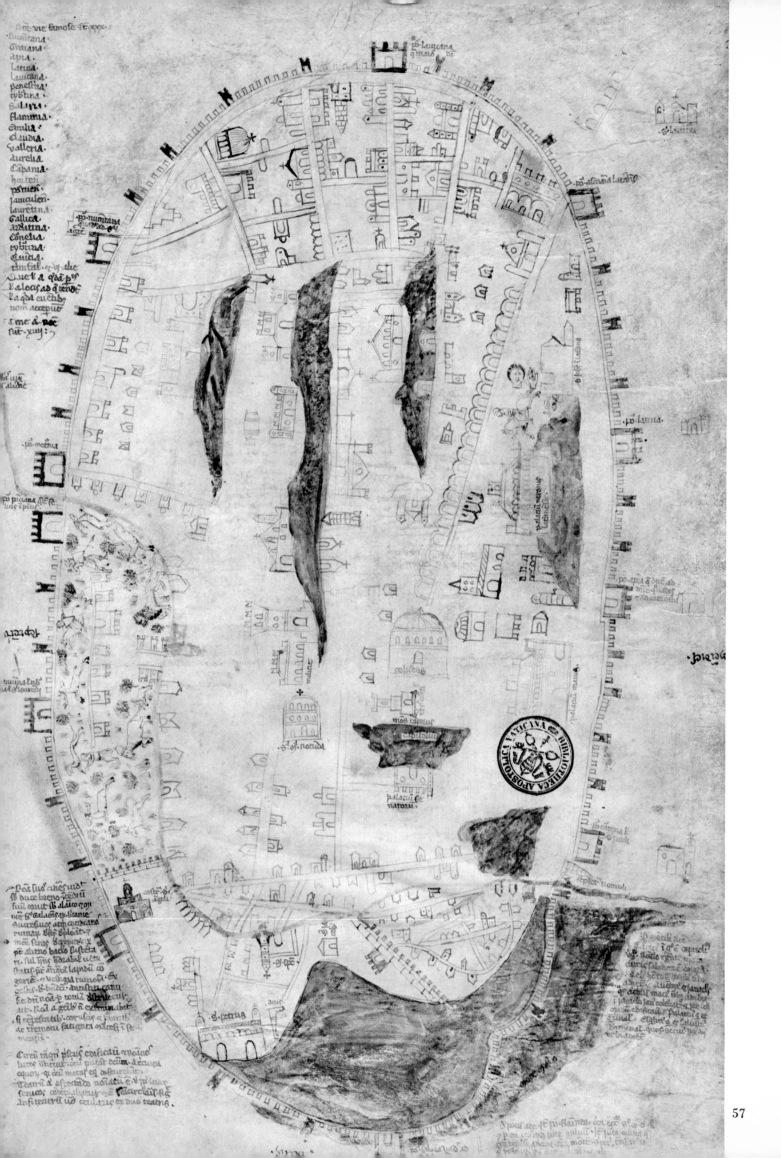

Besides, the popes play their part as princes with gusto. All monarchs award decorations, and all monarchs have marvelled at what men will do for pieces of gold and enamel on a ribbon. The popes give away several sorts of these decorations and I do not doubt that the services for which they are awarded are of a higher moral order than they are in other courts. But a medal is a medal and the man who wants one cannot wish to hide his merits under a bushel. The popes, therefore, have rightly ordained that the recipients of certain orders must pay an initial tax towards the funds of the Church. This is very pragmatical. So, it would appear, are the popes. No lesser an authority than the then (1960) Cardinal Secretary of State has told the story of how, when one day he ventured to whisper into the ear of the drowsing Pope Pacelli that a certain so-and-so would like not to pay the tax, because he was short of cash, the Pope was instantly wide awake and, banging the arm of his chair, said, "No! He must pay!" This pope will one day be made a saint. But, clearly, he was also a monarch. How this came about, forms one of the most interesting chapters in the history of Rome.

3

THE EMPEROR CONSTANTINE DID MORE THAN ANY SINGLE MAN IN history to change the course of European civilisation, but we are quite unable to say why he did it. He gave Christianity its first official sanction: he was deeply interested in the affairs of the church; he intervened in the quarrels between bishops and even claimed that he was a bishop himself—"a bishop of those without the Church." But was he a Christian? Did he believe in Christianity? We cannot say. It is not certain that he was ever baptised. But what is sure is that, if he was received into the Church, it was only on his deathbed. That is to say, we can never know if he was really converted or not. A man on his deathbed is not in a position to argue theology: nor can he subsequently come back and tell us he was tricked into being baptised. He took the Christian faith seriously, in all seeming. But when he was given two of the nails that were supposed to have fixed Christ on the Cross, he put one on the top of a monument (which was a reverent thing to do), and the other he made into a bit for his horse, which was not reverent at all.

Another act of his was equally mysterious. When he decided to transfer the capital of the Empire from Rome to Byzantium, he took with him the whole Court, and many senatorial families. But he left

55 *This primitive fishing-boat traditionally symbolises the power and security of the papacy. The drawing is after a mosaic by Giotto. On the right, St Peter can be seen sinking into the sea, whilst testing his faith in Jesus by trying to walk on water. Jesus is lifting him up.*

56 *Pope Boniface VIII proclaims the Holy Year of 1300 to a small but enthusiastic crowd. This picture is a copy of a large fresco said to have been done by Giotto in the Lateran Palace. The protocol of the honorary tapestry, the retinue of courtiers and the ecclesiastical authorities on either side of the pontiff is still maintained in the 20th century, when the Pope gives a public audience. The only major innovation since those times is the presence of the Court photographer.*

57 *A rudimentary medieval map of Rome showing the major churches and the battlements. It is a 14th-century copy of an earlier map, which probably dated from the early 13th century. The few antique monuments marked are those described in the medieval pilgrims' guide book, the "Mirabilia Urbis Romae", and include the Tomb of Romulus, Palace of Nero and Colosseum, shown with a hemispherical dome.*

behind the body of St Peter and the person of his successor, the Pope. Did he dismiss the whole story of the succession from the Apostle as a priestly fiction? In that case, it is strange that he ordered an enormous basilica to be built over the saint's tomb. Why did he not take the Pope along with all the rest to his new capital?

These are important questions. The honest thing to say, when faced with them, is that we shall never know the answers. But that is something that people have always been reluctant to admit. The actions of Constantine stir up our sense of the drama of history. We are tempted to fill in the gaps in the plot with fabrications. In this case, the gap was filled in with one of the most bare-faced fabrications on record, the Donation of Constantine.

One of the effects of the transfer of the capital of the Empire to Constantinople was that it left the Romans comparatively in peace to think out things for themselves without being under the mighty thumb of the Emperor. We have seen that Roman civilisation had little, if any, originality. The Romans were greedy borrowers of other people's culture. Inevitably, then, the Empire in Byzantium became no longer Roman, but Greek. After a while its manners, its customs and finally its language became incomprehensible to the Romans of Rome. These, now almost entirely Christian, began to look upon themselves as the true heirs of the Empire, however much the Hellenized Byzantines might claim the contrary.

This was particularly true of the popes. They acknowledged the Emperor. But he was a long way away. They looked to him for protection from the barbarians who were increasingly pressing upon them. But the emperors could not always give it. They looked to the emperors for advice in the worldly affairs of the Church, but all too often when it came, it seemed to be merely the outcome of some Court intrigue that the popes had barely heard of and which, in any case, did not bear upon their problems. Increasingly, they felt that they were on their own.

Besides, what exactly was this Christian emperor in a far-off land? He clearly was not the sort of emperor that the pagan rulers had been. He was a Christian, governing Christians, a profoundly different thing from a tyrant governing heathens. As we have seen, the Christian faith changed men's view of history. It provided Rome with a moral reason. It dismissed history before the advent of Christ as unimportant. It stressed hope in the future, which would be essentially a Christian one. The faith was not merely something one practised on Sundays. It permeated everything in living. It controlled every man's conduct.

58 *A miniature from the famous "Pontificale Ottoboniana", a Renaissance manuscript, which is one of the treasures of the Vatican Library. The scene shown is part of the ceremony of the consecration of a bishop. For a time during the Middle Ages, lay princes claimed the right to choose their own prelates. But the popes waged a bitter, and sometimes physically violent, fight against the practice, and won.*

The Emperor was a man. Therefore it controlled the Emperor. If it controlled the Emperor, how was the Emperor to know what the faith really taught? Plainly, he should go to the people who knew best—that is, the priests. The priests were controlled and advised by the High Priest, the Supreme Pontiff. The Supreme Pontiff was the Pope. It followed—according to the popes—as the night follows day that the Pope ought to be the master of the Emperor.

One of the thinkers of the time, Gelasius, who was a pope himself, expressed the essence of the matter very clearly. "The Pope," he said, "was the successor of St Peter and thus had authority over the whole body of the faithful." The Emperor also had his place. It was his duty to look after the carnal and material wants of the popes, so that the popes could give full time to the job of running everything. And to clinch the matter, Gelasius points out that emperors have souls, souls must be saved and nobody can do that for the Emperor but the Pope.

As my narrative thus far has shown, we must entirely agree with Gelasius. We might think the result of the argument preposterous: but the argument itself is perfectly sound. It is also explosive. Gelasius lived in the 5th century. But in the 20th, Monsignor Ronald Knox in a little book about the Church remarked in passing that, logically, in a Catholic country the Pope could insist that the Catholic government obey his wishes. Monsignor Knox, bowing to the storm that this raised, could only say that what he had written was right, but he shouldn't have said it. He was, in fact, merely repeating what Gelasius, a clear-headed man, had said, and what the popes have never—and could never—deny.*

The Roman Emperor, then, had been put in his place. He was under the Pope, and he must take the Pope's orders. Unfortunately, the popes were not in a position to give them, and the Emperor was not inclined to listen. As the Hellenisation of the Empire increased, the Christian Emperor grew more and more to resemble the divine emperor of pagan times. He professed the humble faith of Christ, but in a manner all his own. If he could not consider himself a god, he could insist that he was sacred, which is the next best thing, and quite as satisfying. The imperial palace—including the outhouses—was all sacred, because it contained the throne-room, which looked like a

59 *A corner of the large and beautiful cloister of St Paul Outside-the-Walls. It was begun by the Benedictines in 1193 and finished in 1208. The cloister was the only part of the church which was not destroyed in the 1823 fire.*

* The Church might not give any orders, or the government might decide not to obey those that she did. Further, few countries are now wholly Christian, which complicates matters but does not affect the general truth of Gelasius' argument. For a fuller discussion of the origins of this perennial debate see Walter Ullmann's *The Growth of Papal Government in the Middle Ages.*

church and was super-sacred. In the exedra or niche of this room was a mosaic picturing Christ as God and Man. Immediately under this was the Emperor's elevated throne. God was venerated on feast-days, but so was the Emperor, and the ritual with which this was done was as solemn as a divine service. When he signed documents, he did so with his "divine right hand" and used red ink to mark the fact, a custom copied in recent times by the British viceroys in India. Anybody receiving one of these sacred documents bowed before it and kissed it. If he was actually in the celestial presence of the Emperor himself, he had to fall flat on his face.

The popes were not so lucky. At this time, their election was in the hands of rival factions among the citizens of Rome, and the Romans were not good losers. Pope Formosus, for instance, was elected to the papacy in A.D. 891 He died in A.D. 896. A few years later the faction that had been defeated at his election got their own man on to St Peter's Chair. Formosus was dragged out of his coffin, dressed up in pontifical vestments and put on trial. A trembling deacon, sitting next to the ghastly figure of the accused, was charged with giving the dead pope's answers. These were found wanting and the fingers with which the corpse was accustomed, in life, to give the papal benediction were cut off. The body was then dragged through the streets, pelted by the people and thrown into the Tiber. The faction had admirably made its point that Formosus was the wrong man to be elected. But their own nominee, when, after an interval, he was finally made Pope, had no better fortune. He (Stephen VII) was dethroned in a popular rising and thrown into prison. There the Supreme Pontiff was strangled.

It was ridiculous that men in such a precarious condition could read emperors a lesson: but it was also, in its way, sublime. It has always been one of the virtues of holding a religious faith that it enables one to be insolent to one's betters. In challenging the emperors, the popes showed that the original belief that Christ had come to turn the whole world upside down still flourished. As for the emperors, they first ignored the matter, and when it became impossible they treated the popes as public nuisances. On one occasion emissaries were sent from Byzantium to arrest the pontiff. But the people of Rome, always fickle, instead of beating their pope, thrashed the emissaries, who were forced to give up their mission.

A man who is convinced that he is right, because he has God on his side, can win great victories against almost everybody, except another man who is equally convinced that God is on his side. Then there

60 *In the very ancient Roman church of St Balbina is this tomb of Cardinal Stefano Surdi, which is dated 1303. Note the cosmatesque mosaic work around the base. This system of using circles of coloured marble came into vogue at a time when there were still a large number of antique columns available which could be sliced up, and the slices used for decoration. The church was restored in 1910.*

61

is a stalemate, or war to the knife. In this case, the Emperor was certain that he was every bit as good a Christian as the Pope and obviously, being born to the purple, much more a gentleman. He would not give way, from principle, and besides, he had the big battalions.

The papacy was thus in a dilemma. It could neither coerce the Emperor, nor obey him. This situation might have endured for a long time had not the popes hit upon a solution which was beautiful in its simplicity. They would ignore Byzantium and make another emperor. If it were argued that nobody had ever heard of priests making kings, it could equally well be argued that nobody had ever heard priests using language such as the popes used to crowned heads. Since Gregory II, there could be no going back. The Emperor in Byzantium had written to the Pope to persuade him to destroy religious images to which the Emperor had an objection. Gregory, incensed, had replied as follows:

"We derive our power and authority from the prince of the apostles, Peter, and we could, if we wished, pronounce judgment upon you, but you have already pronounced judgment upon yourself and on your counsellors: and you and they may just as well remain accursed.

"Listen to us, Emperor, cease behaving like a priest, and follow the sacred churches, as you ought. Dogmas are not the business of emperors, but of pontiffs, because we have the sense and mind of Christ ... you, Emperor, cannot have the right mind for dogmas; your mind is too coarse and martial."

And he had summed the matter up:

"If you swagger and threaten us ... we do not wish to enter into a quarrel with you. Three miles away the pope will escape into the Campania [the countryside round Rome], and then good luck to you —you might just as well chase the wind.

"... You know very well that your empire cannot be sure of Roman Italy, except the city of Rome and this only because of the nearness of the sea. But, as I have said, the pope has to move only three miles and he is outside your empire. It is regrettable that the savages and barbarians have become cultured, whilst you as a cultured individual have degraded yourself to the level of the barbarians ... The whole Occident offers the prince of the apostles proofs of faith, and if you should send men to destroy holy images (in the Occident) then I had better warn you: we prophesy to you beforehand that we shall be innocent of the blood that will then flow; this blood may recoil upon you.

"... The whole Occident looks to us, and even if we do not deserve it, the Occidental peoples have great confidence in us and in him whose

61 *A full view of the cloister of St Paul Outside-the-Walls. See Plate 59.*

62 *A bishop's throne in the church of St Balbina, in cosmatesque style.*

images you wish to destroy, that is St Peter, whom all kingdoms of the West venerate like God on earth: if you wish to test this, verily, the peoples of the West are ready."

It is very fine and brave, but it is, of course, whistling in the dark. The peoples of the Occident were, indeed, ready, but whether to defend images or throw the pontiff in the Tiber, no pope could ever be sure. For the irony of the matter was that although the popes claimed to be the masters of the emperor, the master had dire need of the strong right arm of his servant. Unless the popes had a protector, they stood in danger of being destroyed either by the people of Rome or by the Lombards, who hungrily eyed the still great city, and constantly threatened to overwhelm it.

Shortly after this, it happened that the Franks, by now a thoroughly Christian people, were ruled by usurpers. The legitimate kings survived, but were of no consequence. The people were ruled by the chief official of the palace and ruled very well. But the usurpers and their supporters were bound by oath to serve the usurped king. This weighed on the conscience, or the pride, of the acting ruler, Pepin, and he sent ambassadors to Pope Zachary, to ask what was the situation. Were they in reality bound by their oath to the legitimate monarch, a feeble-witted nonentity, or were they free from it? Pope Zachary decided that the legitimate king should be deposed, have his head shaved, and be shut up in a monastery till he was dead. The moral grounds of this decision are obscure; but they need not be investigated since a pope who had the power of the keys of Heaven presumably had power to lock anybody he pleased in a monastery. The practical basis of the affair is plainer. Pepin had the big battalions.

The successor to Zachary, Pope Stephen II, went to France and there anointed Pepin king. He soon had need of the battalions. Rome was threatened by Lombards with siege and sack unless every citizen paid a piece of gold as a ransom. The Pope implored the aid of Pepin, who nobly responded and drove the Lombards away. Unfortunately, they came back. This caused Stephen to write an urgent letter to Pepin: to make sure that it would be taken seriously he wrote in the name of St Peter and signed it accordingly.

In his letter, St Peter is most pressing. Calling the king his son, he assures him that not only he, St Peter, wants him to fight for Rome, but also the Virgin, the angels, the saints and the martyrs. From his uniquely favourable point of vantage, St Peter is able to assure the king that if he does what he is asked, he will go to heaven, and if he does not he will go to hell.

Pepin bowed to the Apostle's wishes and once more saved Rome. Whether he believed, like a good Christian, that St Peter had written the letter or suspected, like a good statesman, that the Pope had had a hand in it, we do not know. In any case, it was a minor fraud. A much greater one was to come.

Some time in the 8th century, an unknown but learned scoundrel concocted what he called the Decretals of Constantine, to which he attached a document called the Donation. It was founded on a sort of dramatic reconstruction of what someone thought would have been a nice thing to happen when Constantine was alive. Taking the dramatic parts of this story (the *Legenda sancti Silvestri*), the forger turned them to his own, or rather the Pope's, ends. Since the reader may never have seen a historical forgery, I shall give some part of it in its own words.

Constantine was a man who fought for, won and brilliantly re-organised the greatest empire in the world. His energy and acumen were such that he was able to transfer its capital to a distant land and there to found and build a city, which remained the capital for eleven hundred and twenty-three years. He successfully negotiated the first and most important steps in changing the faith of his subjects from one of great antiquity to one that was new, foreign and still despised. In addition, he was a man who could handle and dominate quarrelling ecclesiastics in the upper echelons of the hierarchy—by no means the least of his remarkable qualities. The reader may care to judge for himself whether the forgery, purporting to come from such a man, is in any way convincing. He may then reflect on the undoubted fact that it *did* convince.

The Donation of Constantine begins:

"In the name of the holy and undivided Trinity, the Father, the Son and the Holy Spirit. The Emperor Caesar Flavius Constantinus in Christ Jesus (one of the same Holy Trinity our Saviour, Lord and God) faithful, merciful, mighty, beneficent, Alamannicus, Gothicus, Sarmaticus, Germanicus, Brittanicus, Hunicus, pious, fortunate, victorious, triumphant, ever august; to the most holy and blessed father of fathers, Sylvester, Bishop of the Roman city and Pope; and to all his successors, the pontiffs, who shall sit in the chair of blessed Peter to the end of time; as also to all the most reverend and God-beloved Catholic bishops, by this our imperial constitution subjected throughout the world to this same Roman church, whether they be appointed now or at any future time—grace, peace, love, joy, long-suffering, mercy from God the Father Almighty and Jesus Christ His Son and the Holy Spirit be with you all."

The Emperor then goes on to announce to all that he has been converted to Christianity and has renounced the worship of idols. He explains why this happened, and it is this part of the story that was borrowed from the earlier romance.

"For when a horrible and filthy leprosy invaded all the flesh of my body and I was treated by many assembled doctors but could not thereby attain to health, there came to me the priests of the Capitol, who said I ought to erect a font on the Capitol, and fill it with the blood of innocent children and by bathing in it while it was warm I could be healed. According to their advice many innocent children were assembled; but, when the sacrilegious priests of the pagans wished them to be slaughtered and the font filled with their blood, our serenity perceived the tears of their mothers and I thereupon abhorred the project; and, pitying them, we ordered their sons to be restored to them, gave them vehicles and gifts and sent them back rejoicing to their homes. And when the day had passed, and the silence of the night had descended upon us and the time of sleep had come, the apostles Sts. Peter and Paul appeared to me saying: 'Since thou has put an end to thy sins and hast shrunk from shedding the blood of the innocent, we are sent by Christ, our Lord God, to impart to thee a plan for the recovery of thy health. Hear therefore our advice and do whatever we bid thee. Sylvester, bishop of the city of Rome, flying from thy persecutions, is in hiding with his clergy in the caverns of the rocks on Mount Serapte. When thou hast called him to thee, he will show you the pool of piety; and, when he has thrice immersed thee therein, all the strength of this leprosy will leave thee. When that is done, make this return to thy Saviour, that by thy command all the churches throughout the world be restored; and purify thyself in this way, by abandoning all the superstitions of idols and adoring and worshipping the living and true God, who alone is true, and devote thyself to His will.'"

Constantine is duly immersed by Pope Sylvester and is cleansed of his leprosy. Sylvester takes the opportunity to give him a lesson on the foundation of the papacy, quoting the text that is written round the dome of St Peter's, "Thou art Peter," and so forth. Constantine calls together his governors, his senators and the leaders of the people who unanimously decide, in view of the Emperor's cure and, bearing in mind the text, that:

"The sacred See of the blessed Peter shall be gloriously exalted above our empire and earthly throne."

Constantine decrees that this shall be so, adding, with a remarkable

63 *The church of St John and St Paul, which is amongst the oldest in Rome. Built in 398, it was restored in 1154. Recent architectural work has brought to light a 5th-century colonnade and medieval remains. Note, particularly, the elegant romanesque bell-tower, which is founded upon an ancient Roman base of heavy blocks of stone.*

64

knowledge of church politics, that "he shall have rule, as well, over the four principal Sees, Antioch, Alexandria, Constantinople and Jerusalem, and also over all the churches of God in all the world."

St Peter and St Paul, when they had appeared to the Emperor, had merely asked that he be a good Christian and restore the churches. Constantine, however, felt compelled to go further. The document goes on to say that he wishes to give certain gifts to the Apostles Sts. Peter and Paul, to Sylvester, the Pope, and to all his successors. These are:

"Our imperial Lateran palace, which is superior to and excels all palaces in the whole world; and further the diadem which is the crown of our head; and the mitre; as also the super-humeral, that is, the stole which usually surrounds our imperial neck; and the purple cloak and the scarlet tunic and all the imperial robes."

As something of an anticlimax, he adds that the popes shall rank as commanders of the imperial cavalry. But he soon recovers his form. After announcing that all the clergy shall be regarded as patricians and consuls (the last honour being an almost hysterical touch), he goes on to say that:

"Wherefore that the pontifical crown should not be made of less repute, but rather that the dignity of a more than earthly office and the might of its glory should be yet further adorned—lo, we convey to the oft-mentioned and most blessed Sylvester, universal pope, both our palace as preferment, and likewise all provinces, palaces and districts of the city of Rome and Italy and of the regions of the West; and bequeathing them to the power and sway of him and the pontiffs, his successors, we do (by means of fixed imperial decision through this our divine, sacred and authoritative sanction) determine and decree that the same be placed at his disposal, and do lawfully grant it as a permanent possession to the holy Roman Church."

After that the forger could scarcely go further. All that was left was to pack the Emperor off to Byzantium, and have done with him:

"Wherefore we have perceived that our empire and the power of our government should be transferred and removed to the regions of the East and that a city should be built in our name in the best place in the province of Byzantium and that our empire there established; for it is not right that an earthly emperor should have authority there, where the rule of priests and the head of the Christian religion have been established by the Emperor of Heaven . . .

"Given at Rome, March 30th, when our lord Flavius Constantinus, for the fourth time, and Galliganus, most illustrious men, were Consuls."

64 *A view of the Roman Forum as it was for many centuries. The last monument to be raised in the Forum was one to the Byzantine Emperor Phocas in 608. After that the Forum was abandoned. Furnaces were set up to make building-lime out of the marble, and animals were pastured there to such an extent that the Forum was called the "Campo Vaccino", the cow-field. The first systematic archaeological diggings were started in the middle of the 19th century. As can be seen from this picture, there were many columns and buildings which were never lost to the sight of the Romans. This painting, in the Doria Gallery, is by P. Brill of Antwerp and shows the Forum in the 16th century.*

65 *The old Clivus Scauri (the slope of the buttresses) is probably the road of Rome which evokes the medieval period more than any other. On the right is the church of St John and St Paul, two officers of the Imperial court who suffered martyrdom under Julian the Apostate.*

It was now obvious to all right-thinking men that the popes could make emperors how and when they pleased. The man the popes' choice fell upon was at least worthy of the honour. He was Charlemagne, who had already proved himself a powerful and energetic protector of the Church under Pope Adrian I. The next pope was Leo III, whose election surprised and disgusted at least part of the people of Rome. They expressed their opinion in the usual fashion. When he was taking part in a religious procession, he was assaulted, beaten and imprisoned. Here it would appear that his captors threatened to cut out his tongue and his eyes. He lost neither, escaped and ran to Charlemagne. The king accompanied him to Rome, where he first had the idea that Leo should be put on trial in order to prove that the people who had attacked him were in the wrong.

Some theological niceties were brought to the attention of Charlemagne, who then agreed that it was difficult to see who could judge a pope, although it was obvious who could beat him up. Leo was merely asked to defend himself in a public speech. His manner of doing this was to take an oath that anything said against him was untrue, and since he was Pope, he could not, like a secular character in later history, tell a lie. This defence was accepted by Charlemagne, and since Charlemagne's troops were quartered in the city, it was also accepted by the people of Rome.

On Christmas Day, the grateful Pope made Charlemagne a present while Charlemagne was worshipping in St Peter's. The Pope put a crown upon his head and, amid the well-rehearsed acclamation of the congregation, Charles became the Roman Emperor.

Charles affected to be surprised, which is not a probable reaction. But he might well have been puzzled. A man of action, and far from a believer in fairy-tales, he perfectly well knew that there was already a real Roman emperor sitting in majesty in his palace in Constantinople: and Charles had no intention of taking issue with him. But he did not take off the crown. He merely forbore using the title, inventing instead a form of words that would not offend the true emperor. But he had acquiesced in a myth, and the myth proved stronger than the facts. Leo III had picked himself up from the streets of Rome and, by the aid of a forgery, had made an emperor. More, he had founded the Holy Roman Empire, a fiction that was to bedevil European history for centuries. Even today, a great cloak hangs in the Pope's wardrobe ready to be worn by the Holy Roman Emperor, when he listens to Mass in St Peter's. But, fortunately, and at last, there isn't one.

66 *A fresco by Fra Angelico showing St Laurence giving alms to the poor and the maimed, with a background resembling Roman architecture of the time. It is in the private chapel of Nicholas V, which the Pope commissioned Fra Angelico to decorate.*

66

TEMPLA DOMVM EXPOSITIS·VICOS·FORA·MOENIA PONTES·
VIRGINEAM·TRIVII·QVOD·REPARARIS·AQVAM·
PRISCA·LICET·NAVTIS·STATVAS·DARE·COMMODA·PORTVS·
ET·VATICANVM·CINGERE·SIXTE·IVGVM·
PLVS·TAMEN·VRBS·DEBET·NAM·QVAE·SQVALORE·LATEBAT·
CERNITVR·IN·CELEBRI·BIBLIOTHECA·LOCO·

IT IS GENERALLY BELIEVED THAT IT IS THE COMMON PEOPLE WHO embrace a myth and build it up until it is more real than the facts. But that is only partly true. The populace is fickle. For instance, the myth of Britain's imperial destiny grew up among the broad masses of England. It was nurtured in the music-hall and the popular press. But nobody arose to head the movement, except evanescent politicians. At last, when Churchill remarked with dismay that he did not conceive it to be his duty to give away the British Empire, he found that this was precisely the job that he had to do, because nobody cared. The people of England were thinking of other matters, other fairy-tales, in particular the one which said everybody could be rich without doing any work. And we have seen that in the case of the legend of the austerity of the Roman character, the people barely took any notice of it, unless it was forced upon them by the priests, the thinkers and the writers. The great delusions of history have all had brains behind them. Nor are the intellectuals who propagate them necessarily dishonest. It is the weakness of all people with keen intelligences that they will go to great lengths to avoid admitting that they have been fools. The extraordinary language of present-day Marxist theoreticians is a case in point. It is not, as some superficial people say, double-talk and double-think. It is not deception. It is the product of immensely active intelligences who cannot admit that they are wrong and who do not, after due thought and argument, see that they are. In the ancient world, the grim nonsense of Plato in his *Laws* and *Republic* are instances of the same thing, while in the Orient, the more extravagant doctrines of Hinduism are the product of centuries of labours by most subtle minds caught in a similar trap.

The fabrication of the right of the popes to make emperors and the creation of a "new" Roman Empire might have died from its very excess of absurdity, had it not been for one powerful intelligence. The broad mass of Catholics seem to have been uninterested in it. Their attitude towards all priests from the Pope downwards was what it has always been in Catholic Europe. That is, they looked upon them as men who prevented the people's pleasures and made money out of their sorrows, but without whom there can be no practical faith. Romans continued to abuse the popes, even when they were king-makers, and kings continued to quarrel with them.

The empire of Charlemagne broke up at his death and for a time Europe was ruled by princelings. Then one man, Otho, rose above

67 *A picture of Sixtus IV, who founded the Vatican Library, appointing his librarian. The artist is Melozzo da Forli (1438-94).*

his rivals. Needing some way of making this plain without fighting everybody who cared to contradict him, he turned to the Pope. The gimcrackery of the new Roman Empire was used to confirm him and his successors in their positions. It was taken for what it was worth, and no more.

But then, in 1073, a man of vast energy, penetrating mind and resolute character, called Hildebrand, came to the papacy, taking the title of Gregory VII. He had already been instrumental in reforming the manners and morals of the priesthood. He had inspired the important change in the manner of electing popes which excluded the people for ever from interfering and put the choice in the hands of the cardinals. Now, bringing his powerful intelligence to bear upon the authority of the papacy, he proceeded to take the claims of the Donation of Constantine with utter seriousness, and set about forcing them down the throats of every Christian king. He excommunicated one of them, and the result is one of the few things in this business of popes and emperors that is taught in schools. Henry IV stood in the snow for three days at Canossa to persuade the Pope to pardon him. Something of the temper of Gregory can be caught in his own description of what happened, as he made it in a speech at the synod of March 1080.

"(Henry) came to me in Lombardy begging me to release him from excommunication. And when I had witnessed his humility and when he had promised me reforms of his life, I restored him to communion only, but *I did not re-instate him in his kingship* from which I had deposed him in the Roman synod."

These are tremendous words. Clearly they are spoken by a man who firmly believes he has the supreme power on earth, a man who is certain that, in his own words, "if the See of St Peter decides and judges celestial things, how much more does it decide the earthly and secular."

In 1075, a Roman noble, Cencio, who had no love for Hildebrand, maintained, with sound historical knowledge, that if anybody was going into the business of making Roman emperors, it should be the people of Rome, who alone had the right to do so.

Taking it upon himself to represent them, he offered the imperial crown to a Norman adventurer, Robert Guiscard. Feeling sure of Guiscard's support, he next instigated a conspiracy. While the Pope was celebrating Mass in St Mary Major's on Christmas night, Cencio, accompanied by a group of armed men invaded the church and kidnapped the Pope. Having wounded Gregory in the head in the course of the scuffle, he flung the Pope across his horse, still in his vestments, and carried him off. He shut him up in a tower. But the Roman populace, taking offence at having one of its favorite ceremonies interrupted, stormed the tower, released Gregory, and carried him still bleeding back to St Mary Major where, after the lapse of a day, he finished his Mass.

With Gregory's subsequent adventures and misfortunes, we cannot be concerned here. But before he died in exile, he had elevated the claims—or the conceit—of the papacy so far that the Pope not only made emperors, but himself assumed the imperial pomp. We have seen that in the Donation the Emperor gaves the Pope his crown and his regalia. From now on, popes in procession will be dressed like emperors, as indeed they still are. They will wear a crown: they will wear a red cape, because the imperial garments were always red. They will be surrounded by a Court, and the principal courtiers, who are cardinals, will publicly do obeisance in the most humble manner before their masters.

All the world saw the crowning of Pope John XXIII. Most of it thought, under the tutelage of the newspaper correspondents, that he was being crowned Pope. But popes do not need a crown. John XXIII, an hour before his crowning, had already taken his place upon the throne of St Peter. He had already, as Supreme Pontiff and St Peter's successor, said Mass at the papal altar over the Apostle's tomb. His cardinals had already twice done obeisance before him. Then, and only then, as the acknowledged Pope, did he go to the balcony of the basilica and permit a cardinal to place a crown on his head.

The Donation of Constantine has long ago been denounced by the Church itself as a forgery. Popes no longer claim to make kings, nor do they give kings orders. Still, Pope Roncalli is a king himself and cannot escape it. We have seen why.

The Renaissance reviewed PART FOUR

1

ONE OF THE OBVIOUS REASONS WHY HISTORY IS LESS THAN HALF-
true is that we have not enough facts. There is another. Even when we
know sufficient facts, we sometimes choose to ignore them. This is
because most of us have a period in history in which, according to our
view, people lived and died, fought and ruled, solely to prove a point
in which we are particularly interested and about which we hold very
firm opinions. Thus each of us is not only inescapably ignorant of
whole stretches of history, in addition each of us has his own personal
view of history, coloured by his politics, his religion and his temperament. Some of the most stimulating and dramatic periods of history
have been largely the invention of men of strong prejudices and literary
ability. The Renaissance is a case in point.

For some highly intelligent, but prejudiced people, the history of
Europe is Christian to the point of monotony. Since they do not like
the Christian religion (or, maybe, the Catholic version of it), they are
happy whenever, in the history of Europe, Christianity has a set-back.
They feel warmly towards a man like Julian the Apostate (who tried
to revive paganism) because they feel that, put into an emperor's
scarlet shoes, that is exactly the thing they would have done themselves.
Now, in the 15th century there was a revival of interest in Roman and
Greek things in Italy and, to such people, it is a god-send. In writing
and thinking about it, they feel that they are throwing open the
windows of innumerable airless sacristies, unbarring the doors of
gloomy convents and letting the fresh air blow away the smell of
candles and incense. They feel as invigorated by the Renaissance as a
good housewife by a day's spring-cleaning in her husband's study.
They draw a picture for us of an Italy sunk in religious torpor, suddenly being awakened by a few enterprising spirits who, in turn, inspired

68 *A detail from a fresco by Pinturicchio
showing St Catherine of Alexandria
disputing with philosophers in front of the
Emperor Maximian. The saint is dressed
in the blue and red of the Borgia family,
and her features are said to be those of
Lucrezia Borgia, whose reputation of
ill-fame is now believed to be quite
unjustified. The fresco is in the Borgia
Apartments of the Vatican.*

69

70

a number of gifted artists, who in turn set the tone of a new, free-thinking, liberated society which lasted until the Christian religion, by devious and detestable means, once more put out the light.

This view was particularly popular fifty years ago, when everybody who had any claim to be an intellectual was liberating everybody else from everything. Since educators, who at all costs must feel sure of themselves, prefer to remain some fifty years behind the times in their information, this picture of the Renaissance is the one which most of us acquired at school and at college. It has been so drummed into us that it has become a commonplace to deplore the modern Italians. How, it is asked, can a nation that once burst so suddenly into wonderful creativeness do nothing now except design slick automobiles? Has the effort exhausted them? Will they astonish us again by another flare-up? We devoutly hope so and we watch intently for any sign of it. Just after the second world war, great pressure was brought to bear by intellectuals all over the world to make the modern Italians take the lead in culture once again. The Italians, who are an obliging people, did their best and produced an original line in beach pants for women.

The truth is that the really astonishing thing about the Renaissance is the length of time the Italians spent before they did anything about it, even though the thing was held under their noses. But then, the Italians (once the Roman Empire disappeared) were slow at accepting foreign things, as they still are: and the rebirth of learning was not Italian at all. It was Arabian.

2

WHEN ST FRANCIS OF ASSISI WAS GIVEN A BEAUTIFULLY ILLUMI-nated manuscript of the gospels, he tore out the pages and gave one to each of his companion friars so that all, he said, somewhat dis-ingenuously, could enjoy it. When Brother Juniper used his sheet to wrap up some greasy food in the kitchen, the saint had no objection at all.

This is the proper Christian attitude towards culture. For the worship of God—and that is a Christian's major concern—it is necessary that some clerics should be learned. Religious pictures are an aid to prayer, so it is necessary that there should be people who know how to paint them. Ecclesiastics should know some history, otherwise the point of certain aspects of the faith—for instance, the Donation of

69 *This is a detail of a large composition by Botticelli showing Moses and the daughters of Jethro. It is on the left wall of the Sistine Chapel. In 1483 Pope Sixtus IV commissioned Perugino, Ghirlandaio, Signorelli, Rosselli and Botticelli to decorate the walls of the Sistine Chapel.*

70 *Another detail of Pinturicchio's huge composition representing St Catherine and the Emperor Maximian (see Plate 68). It shows a group of people listening to St Catherine as she speaks to the philosophers.*

Constantine—would be missed. But culture must not be acquired for its own sake, and religious art cannot be admired for anything but the lesson it teaches. Studies may be pursued, but only to strengthen the arguments for Christianity. St Thomas Aquinas was a man of towering culture and vast learning. But every word of his gigantic output of books is devoted to proving that the Christian religion is true. Nor is there the faintest spirit of inquiry. He begins his argument with the fact that *of course* it is true. Theology, which must be the main study of a Christian, can never be wrong, because its basic assumption is that it is right.

All this is most reasonable. As we have seen, the advent of Christ and his death put an end to history as it was known. It began a new era in which it was his followers' duty to prepare themselves for the Kingdom of Heaven and to enter it if they could. A wide knowledge of, say, books could only be a hindrance. What would you gain by it but an acquaintance with false prophets? As for works of art, they should be made—or at least paid for—prayerfully. Their purpose and not their beauty was the thing which counted in heaven. Occasionally a great work of art would be produced, but not with that intention. Everything in a gothic cathedral was intended to lead the worshippers to thoughts of heaven or fear of hell. It is not quite true that we do not know the names of the architects who built them: we do know some. But apart from their cathedral-building, in which they were overseers of labour rather than architects, they were utterly obscure men.*

In a word, Christians must be good and let who will be clever. But one practical difference between being good and being sinful is that the former is more tiring. In the middle of the Middle Ages, people of means and leisure suffered from a mental disease known as *taedium vitae,* a melancholy in which nothing seemed worthwhile, neither war nor love, money nor fame. There were various means of escape from it. The most civilised place in Europe was the Court of Burgundy and there men and women spent their time in elaborating a Court ritual that had to be meticulously observed every day. At other times immense banquets were given with surprises and entertainments which strike us now as jejune. One has survived in a nursery rhyme:

---

* In an essay of much brilliance, *Gothic Architecture and Scholasticism*, Erwin Panowsky has shown that even the elevations and ground-plans of cathedrals were related to theological arguments. The Spanish Steps (see plate 107) are a curious 18th-century survival of this practice.

71 *The Papal Chancellery is one of the architectural masterpieces of the early Renaissance. It was begun about 1483 and finished in 1511. The architect is not known. The building is often attributed to Bramante, but it is now thought that Andrea Bregno did most of the work. This photograph shows the first-floor loggia in the courtyard.*

72

"Four and twenty blackbirds were baked in a pie.
When the pie was opened
The birds began to sing,
Oh, what a dainty dish to set before the king!"

It was scarcely dainty, but it *was* set before the ruler. The pie was enormous and the "blackbirds" were singers and musicians who emerged from it when the crust was broken, and performed. Elsewhere in Europe, men played complicated games of knights and ladies. In these, courts of "lovers" (who were forbidden to make any love at all) met to draw up rules for being enamoured and tried "offenders" against them, sentencing them to perform tasks for their ladies. But such frippery could not be called artistic and the people who wasted their time on them were not cultured. They were refined, perhaps, but that is a different, and a dreadful, thing.

Nowadays, while still partly Christian, we are very cultured indeed. On my next excursions in Rome I was much exercised on this point. I will not stop to describe the things I went to see. The reader may see them for himself by turning the pages of this book. But, during the time when I was observing the court in the Vatican Palace, I had grown used to walking through its frescoed and gilded rooms without giving them a second glance. If sometimes I was there in the afternoon, I would go through the empty Sistine Chapel in the same way. Then, one morning, while standing in one of the great halls of the palace, a door was opened and I saw the Sistine Chapel with its morning-time public. They were crammed together as if they were at an open-air meeting and listening to a speaker who was suspended above their heads. Since they were all looking at Michelangelo's ceiling (with an occasional studious look at their guide-books), it was possible to study their expressions without offence. I did this, and I did it several times again on other occasions. The level of culture reflected upon these earnest faces was deeply impressive.

It was impressive, and yet a puzzle. It roused me to ask questions. Why should we be cultured? Why should we admire the arts? Why should we cultivate our taste for them? They play so small a part in our way of life that it is notoriously difficult for anyone practising them to make a living. When Mr T. S. Eliot described a room in which women talked of Michelangelo, every reader immediately identified the females as those belonging to a tiny minority, which one generally avoids. The finer things of life play so little part in commerce —which is our main activity—that there is a place in Aspen, Colorado where businessmen can go and find out what they are all about. But,

72 *A side view of the exterior of the Papal Chancellery shown in Plate 71, showing the entrance to the palace's chapel, San Lorenzo in Damaso, which was built by Bramante.*

73 *The 'Tempietto' by Bramante in the courtyard of the church of San Pietro in Montorio on the Janiculum Hill. The church was erected in the 9th century on the spot where it was erroneously thought that St Peter had been crucified. This little temple was built in 1502. It has sixteen Doric columns and was considered by Bramante's contemporaries a masterpiece of architectural interpretation of the classic spirit. Bernini re-used Bramante's design in making the ciborium for the Chapel of the Sacrament in St Peter's.*

74 A portrait of the Florentine Medici Pope Leo X with two of his cardinals; the one on the left, Giulio de' Medici, was later to become Pope Clement VII. The other is Luigi de' Rossi, the Pope's nephew. Painted by Raphael, the picture is now in the Uffizi Gallery in Florence.

75-77 Michelangelo painted the Last Judgment between 1535 and 1541. Plate 75 shows Jesus condemning evil-doers to hell. On his immediate right is Mary: on his left is St Peter holding two large keys. Other figures can be identified as John the Baptist, St Andrew, St Laurence, St Bartholomew and St Sebastian. This enormous picture was divided into eleven sections. Two at the top show angels: below them are two side-sections of saints and martyrs; and the centre-piece is of Christ the Judge with the Madonna, apostles and prophets. Below this, on the left, are the elect being raised up by angels; a centre-section shows angels with trumpets, and on the right are the condemned being pushed back into hell. Below these is Charon, the infernal ferryman, driving sinners into Hades, and to the left is a grotto of demons, and the dead awakening. Plate 76 shows Charon, and Plate 77 a lost soul being carried into hell and peeping at it fearfully with only one eye.

78 The Sistine Chapel. It was built at the time of Sixtus IV between 1473-81, and has been used for electing popes in conclave and other important ceremonies since then. Above the altar is Michelangelo's celebrated Last Judgment. The whole ceiling was frescoed by Michelangelo between 1508 and 1512 and represents the Creation of the World, the Fall of Man and the hopeful signs of redemption. More than twenty years later Michelangelo painted the Last Judgment, behind the altar. It was ordered by Clement VII and painted during the reign of Paul III. The door to the right leads to the Vatican Museum and that to the left to rooms where the Pope keeps his private treasure and personal vestments. On occasion (especially on the day of his election) the Pope vests there. The frescoes on the walls are by such masters as Botticelli, Signorelli, Pinturicchio, Ghirlandaio and Perugino. There are six on each side: subjects from the Old Testament are on the Gospel side (that is to say, on the left looking at the altar), and subjects from the New Testament are on the Epistle side.

79 In the Paolina Chapel (1537, by Antonio Sangallo the Younger), a rarely-used private chapel close to the Sistine, there are two large frescoes by Michelangelo. This picture shows a detail of the crucifixion of St Peter.

80 A detail from one of the thirty frescoes on the ceiling of the Sistine Chapel showing an angel and the prophet Ezekiel.

82

85

83

86

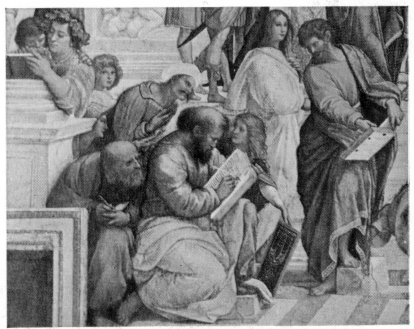

84

87

88

81 *The Miraculous Draught of Fishes.*
This is one of ten tapestries representing
the Acts of the Apostles which were
intended to adorn the Sistine Chapel. They
were woven from designs of Raphael.
Vatican Gallery.

82-87 *The Raphael Rooms were first*
constructed and decorated for Pope
Nicholas V, but it was Julius II who, on
Bramante's recommendation, had Raphael
paint over the previous frescoes. Raphael
started work on these rooms in 1508 at the
age of 24. Plates 82-87 are all in the
Stanza della Segnatura, that is to say, the
Tribunal Room. These Raphael Rooms
are, in fact, in the Vatican Museum, but
the Pope occasionally uses them for private
receptions: and when the see of St Peter is
vacant during a conclave, they are used as
a dining-room for cardinals. In Plate 82,
Apollo plays the viola surrounded by
Muses. Below on either side are members
of the literary profession, amongst whom
are Sappho, Petrarch, Homer, Dante,
Virgil, Boccaccio and Ariosto. Plate 83 is
a detail of Apollo and the Muses. Plate 84
is The Triumph of the Faith or, as it is
sometimes called, The Disputation on the
Most Holy Sacrament. This shows the
Trinity, the Madonna, Adam, saints and
prophets in heaven, and the Church
Militant below worshipping God in the
form of the Eucharist. The School of
Athens is shown in Plate 85. This
represents an ideal gathering of philosophers
in an idealised basilica of Bramante's
design. Plato and Aristotle are in the centre
and Heraclitus sits alone on the steps. Plato
has the face of Leonardo da Vinci and
Heraclitus the features of Michelangelo.
Plate 86 shows Euclid bending down and
taking a measurement: his face is that of the
architect Bramante. Plate 87 represents the
philosopher Pythagoras.

88 *The Transfiguration, which was the*
last major work of Raphael, is in the
Vatican Gallery. It was painted between
1518 and 1520 for Cardinal Giulio de'
Medici. Raphael died before finishing the
picture: he had, however, completed the
composition. The bottom half of the picture
was painted by Giulio Romano and other
of Raphael's assistants. Saints Peter, James
and John are lying on the top of Mount
Tabor, blinded by the light as Christ is
transfigured in front of them. Other
disciples and followers remain at the foot of
the mountain, half-aware of what is
happening. In the right foreground is the
"lunatick and sore vexed" boy, out of whom
Jesus drove the devil.

even there, the realistic organiser is careful to include in the curriculum a considerable amount of special physical exercises designed to improve the figure.

But there is no doubt that we do think that we ought to be cultured. We underpay the people who teach us what it is; we starve the men who produce it, and we would not dream of electing a genuinely creative genius to any public office whatever. In all this, we are at one with the Middle Ages. But we think that culture is a very fine thing and they did not. When did we, in Europe, change?

3

IT IS MY CUSTOM, WHEN THINKING ABOUT ANY HISTORICAL MATTER, to note down the main events in the country that concerns me, and then in parallel columns to list things that happened at the same time in the rest of the world. This is necessary because historians (and they nowadays know it) have the weakness of being very much attached to their parish pump.

The reader will recall that we followed the adventures of Pope Stephen in making Pepin a king. This took place at the beginning of the 9th century. Drawing up my columns for this time and the times near it, I came across a name that must be among the most evocative in history. Between 786 and 809 A.D., Baghdad was under the rule of the Caliph Haroun-al-Raschid.

Everyone knows *The Arabian Nights,* and I suppose part of its fascination for all of us is the way of life it describes. The trappings are splendid—silks, brocades, precious gems, utensils of silver and gold, fountains, courtyards and retinues of servants. The manners of the people are suave, their life is leisured and varied with travel and fine talk. It is all very civilised.

But *The Arabian Nights,* apart from the fantasy, are a truthful and minute description of the way of life in Baghdad at the time of Haroun. This can be glimpsed in the versions that are generally on sale in English. But the real book can be read in French, either in the decent version of Galland or in others less proper. Indeed, the description of the life and pleasures of Baghdad is so true to nature that the full *Arabian Nights* are considered by those who know what is good for us not only unsuitable for children, but unsuitable for any Englishman or American whatsoever. They fear we shall be corrupted. In fact, the Arabs corrupted us all, seven long centuries ago.

89 *A view by night of the Palazzo Senatorio on the Capitoline Hill. It was built on top of the ancient Roman "tabularium", the depository of the Roman archives. The steps which lead to the main entrance are by Michelangelo, but the building itself is by Giacomo della Porta and Girolamo Rainaldi. Below the steps are statues representing Minerva, the Nile and the Tiber.*

90

IMP·CAESARI·DIVI·ANTONINI·DIVI·HADRIANI
NEPOTI·DIVI·TRAIANI·PARTHICI·PRONEPOTI·DIVI
NERVAE·ABNEPOTEM·AVRELIO·ANTONINO·PIO
AVG·GERM·SARM·PONT·MAX·TRIB·POT·XXVII
IMP·VI·COS·III·P·P· · S·P·Q·R

91

In the beginning, Islam was a stern faith, calling for a simple life devoid of all luxuries. Mohammed himself was a man of austere habits and he intended that his followers should be men with soldierly tastes. Their duty was to fight for the faith, and pray. If they did both well— and that meant praying five times a day and dying on the field of battle—they would go to heaven. There, it is true, he promised them a long repose on silken couches and houris to minister to their pleasures, and this has been the cause of a good deal of misunderstanding, especially among people who do not like Muslims and have not read the Koran. But the actual passage is short and almost casual. By and large, the Koran, on the subject of women (the houris were to be in female shape), is discouraging. While permitting more than one wife, as was the Arab custom, it dwells at length on the difficulties of managing them. It recommends that a Muslim take no more than two or three, who must all be treated equally in everything, including frocks and gifts of jewellery. This is an injunction which would give pause to any man of limited means, and in fact the Arabs were, at first, not well off, nor had they any great desire for wealth and comfort.

The early caliphs lived simple lives, dressing in rough woollen robes and living on the coarsest food. On one occasion, the caliph, coming upon some young men of his army who had dressed themselves in some captured silks, got down from his horse, snatched up handfuls of mud and pelted them with it, abusing them at the top of his voice. The faith had no use for popinjays: it wanted hardy fighting men and, for a while, that is what the Arabs were.

But they won too quickly. Kingdoms toppled so rapidly before them that it seemed as though one knocked down another in the course of its fall. Soon the Arabs were masters from Persia to Spain. The hardy fighter was no longer needed, or if he were, the Arabs were so rich he could be bought in the numbers that were required. The Arabs relaxed to enjoy the pleasures of empire.

They were not like the Romans. They were capable of building up their own culture, so markedly individual that the world of Islam still, to this day, seems romantically strange to us in everything from its manners and morals to its architecture. It was a very worldly culture. There was no reason why it should not have been. Islam teaches that a man's overriding duty is to submit to the will of God. God made the world and He obviously intends that it should be lived in. The Mohammedan does so, enjoying it whenever he can, and not complaining when he cannot. Submission to the will of God does not call for self-improvement. The Christian scales moral heights, the better to glimpse the Promised Land; he knows that only the pure in heart will enter the Kingdom of Heaven. Mohammed, who was a practical statesman, was aware that to ask his followers to go out and fight like demons and then come back to their tents with pure hearts and elevated principles would be to show little knowledge of the arts of war. Mothers and wives in modern Western democracies believe that it is possible, but few others do. Mohammed had no such illusions and the Koran has little moral censoriousness or exhortation. It is a work of theology on the nature and omnipotence of God. It is remarkably free from cant of any sort, which is one of the reasons it has never appealed to the taste of the Western world as a book of religion.

But the Koran was all-important in shaping the Muslim way of life. It was not written by Mohammed, who maintained all his life that he was unable to write. It was written by an angel on the shoulder-blades of a sheep, which Mohammed threw higgledy-piggledy into a box. The book as we have it now is a piecing together of these fragments made after Mohammed's death. But the angel was obviously an angel with considerable intellectual equipment. The Bible is an emotional book. The Koran, though much less readable, strikes one as a brainy book. The Bible is not continuously sublime: on the contrary, it is often very earthy and full of human touches that at times move the reader with a purely mundane compassion. The Koran maintains itself on a lofty level of argument. Its human scenes are scarce. It is a continuous demonstration of the aspects of godhead, interwoven with intelligent and moderate advice as to how a sensible, thinking man should conduct himself. It calls for a Muslim to use his head rather than his heart.

It may be for this reason that the culture of the Arabs was an intensely intellectual one, as well as being, in another aspect, sensual. The Arabs called themselves the People of the Book and, from the beginning, learning was highly valued. The Koran, which was very difficult to understand, had to be explained in detail, otherwise there was no Muslim faith. Mohammed did not claim to be divine. He is not worshipped. He left no elaborate ritual behind him, and virtually no supernatural legends. There were only the things that the angel told him, and they had to be interpreted by theologians who must be creative scholars.

Thus while the Christian St Francis tore books to pieces, the Muslims held books in great reverence. They wrote them. They collected them. They read them avidly. Among the books that they collected were the works of the Greeks and the Latins, or such of them as remained after the neglect and, sometimes, the contempt of ages.

The Arabs translated these books into Arabic and collected them in libraries. In the 10th century, when a Christian church could get along on three books for its services, every Muslim mosque had its own library, properly arranged and catalogued. What is more, they were condensed into encyclopaedic works that had great popularity. Masoudi, an industrious compiler who lived in the late 10th century, wrote a compendium of world history and world geography, called *The Plains of Gold and Mines of Precious Stones,* in which are contained capsule histories of Islam, Christianity, the Roman Empire, the Arab Empire, the Jews, the Chinese, the Persians, the Syrians, the Egyptians, the Negroes, the Franks, the Lombards and others. With these histories is a summary of geography, theology, architecture and astronomy.* Turning its pages today, one is struck by the intellectual vivacity of its writer, his openness of mind and his gigantic range of information.

One result of this passion for books was the rebirth of science. Ptolemy was rediscovered and the Arabs made a map of the world, a thing almost as marvellous in that time as our own photographs of the terrestrial sphere and the other side of the moon. And in 830, at a time when everybody in Europe, save a few erudite monks, believed that the world was flat, Al-Ma'mun, an Arabian astronomer estimated the circumference of the world as 24,000 miles and the diameter as 6,500 miles. Nor did the Arabs, in search of knowledge, stop at the Greeks— that was left to the age of classical scholarship in Europe, an age from which we are only now struggling free. They ransacked the libraries of Persia and learned how to write poetry. They studied the writings of the Hindus—something which the Hindus today recoil from doing— and, out of that labyrinth, extracted mathematics. Al-Khwarizmi was the first exponent of the way to use numerals and the first to adopt the Hindu invention of the zero. He worked in the first half of the 9th century, and our numbers are still called "Arabic"—the ones that are useful that is, to distinguish them from the Roman, which are far too clumsy.

To live fully in this world you must be well and, although illness is the will of God and must be patiently endured as such, there is nothing in the Koran to stop a man from trying to get better. The

* It has been translated into French by C. Barbier de Maynard under the title *Les Prairies d'Or.*

Arabs avidly studied every scrap of knowledge they could collect in their vast empire about the arts of healing. From these, the surgeon Abu-al-Quasim compiled a book of medicine which was used, translated, in Europe for centuries.

But although the Arab culture was founded on books, and in particular one book, it was not bookish. It was rich in the graces of living. Rugs, tapestries, and carpets were in use when European princes were still shuffling through rushes on the floors of their *donjons*. Sugar, sherbets and sweetmeats, often mentioned in the *Arabian Nights*, were things which the Crusaders brought back with them as travellers' wonders and were as much, or more, appreciated than the dubious religious relics which were also in their baggage. Washing, too, might be considered a gift to the West from the Arabs. The Muslim faith makes cleanliness an essential part of worship. The Crusaders, who fought the Arabs because they were ungodly, admitted when they came home that the Christians were unwashed.

It is difficult for us today, who have been indoctrinated with the belief that all cultures other than the Western are inadequate, to put ourselves in the place of men and women in the early Middle Ages when faced with a glittering, vigorous civilisation in which everything seemed to be better done, except religion. A Western person who adopts Eastern ways today is a crank. But in the time of which I am writing, Western civilisation had not yet decided that it would collapse unless everybody did the same as everybody else. The Middle Ages were more various, more individual and more ready to change than any subsequent age except that of the High Renaissance. Only religion was static, and even there it was not dead to outside influences. The first Latin translation of the Koran (which was made in the 12th century) was not made by a rebellious heretic or an apostate. It was sponsored by the Abbot of Cluny, Peter the Venerable, along with a number of other Arabic studies. The writings of Ibn-Rushd, known to the West as Averroës, were prescribed reading at the University of Paris.

We tend to think of the Arab Empire (if we can get above the foggy canyons of our education and think about it at all) as being separated from the thresholds of Europe by the expanse of the Mediterranean. But that is not so. The Arabs were across the threshold and comfortably installed in the front hall. By 715 they had conquered Southern Spain and by 902 they were the masters of Sicily. In Cordova, they built a capital that rivalled Baghdad itself. It was served with aqueducts (while those of Rome were falling into ruin); its half-a-million inhabitants enjoyed the luxury of paved streets, which were lit at

93 *This print (by Cavallieri) shows Pope Gregory XIII opening the Holy Year of 1575. He is in the middle distance being carried on the gestatorial chair, under a "baldacchino", towards the portico of the Constantine basilica. Also to be observed, in its correct place in the atrium, is the pine-cone from Hadrian's Mausoleum. In the background, the dome of St Peter's is under construction. Michelangelo had died in 1564, leaving the dome completed only as far as the drum. It was finished in 1590 by Giacomo della Porta and Domenico Fontana.*

FABRICA · S · PETRI · BASILICÆ · NOVA

Illustrissimo et Reuer.mo Domino,
D. Ludouico Madrucio · S · R · E · Cardina
li, Protectori Germaniæ, in perpetuum
subiectionis et obseruantiæ monimentum

Joannes Baptista de Caualleriis Tridentinus D · D ·

PALATII PONTIFICII PARS.

FRONTISPICIVM BASILICÆ · S · PETRI VETI

DOMVS CARD · ARCHIPRESBITERI · S · PETRI

DOMVS CAPELÆ IVLIÆ

PORTICVS CONSTANTINIANA.

SYMMACHI PONS.

En tibi ponimus ob oculos, CHristiane lector, cum sua germana topographia, solennem illam, totiusq. CHristiani orbis concursu nobilitatam, Cerimoniam: quæ uigesimo
quinto quoque anno redeunte, quem Jobileum uocant, in augustissima S. Petri Apostoli Vaticana Basilica, Romæ peragi solita, in Gregorij XIII.
Opt. et felicis. Pontificis tempora incidit: qui, die Natalem Christianum præcedente, desideratum Anno Jobileo principium, daturus, in impluuium suæ atrium
Basilicæ, ipsamq. Porticum Constantinianam, longo ordine præuntibus cum accensis cereis R.mis S · R · E · Cardinahbus, Patriarchis, Archiepiscopis, et Episcopis, habitu Pon
ficio uestitis, descendens Porta, quam Sanctam uulgo dicunt, aperta, signum dedit hoc acceptabili tempore. Orbi Christiano, uiam, ad sananda etiam grauiora conscientiæ uul
ueniamq. peccatorum apud Deum, obtinendam, esse patefactam. Hunc igitur thesaurum, quem Ecclesia mater offert, ut et tu possis acquirere, omni studio. Christiane lector
contende: et de peccatis, per ueram cordis contritionem, oris confessionem, operis satisfactionem expiandis, seriam cogitationem suscipe. Confirmabit, ut ait sanctus ill
Pater, sententia cœli, sententiam Petri, si ad impetrandam delictorum tuorum ueniam, in fide recta, spe firma, Charitateq. non ficta accesseris. Quæ cura ut altius in
animo tuo resideat, typum hunc ante oculos habeto: et in terrena uisibiliq. Cerimonia, quam tibi industria et labore suo. Joannes Baptista de Caualleriis
hic repræsentat, cœlestia inuisibiliaq. mysteria contemplare. Romæ V. Calend. Febr. Anno Jobilei M · D · LXXV.

Cum priuilegio summi Pontificis ad triennium.

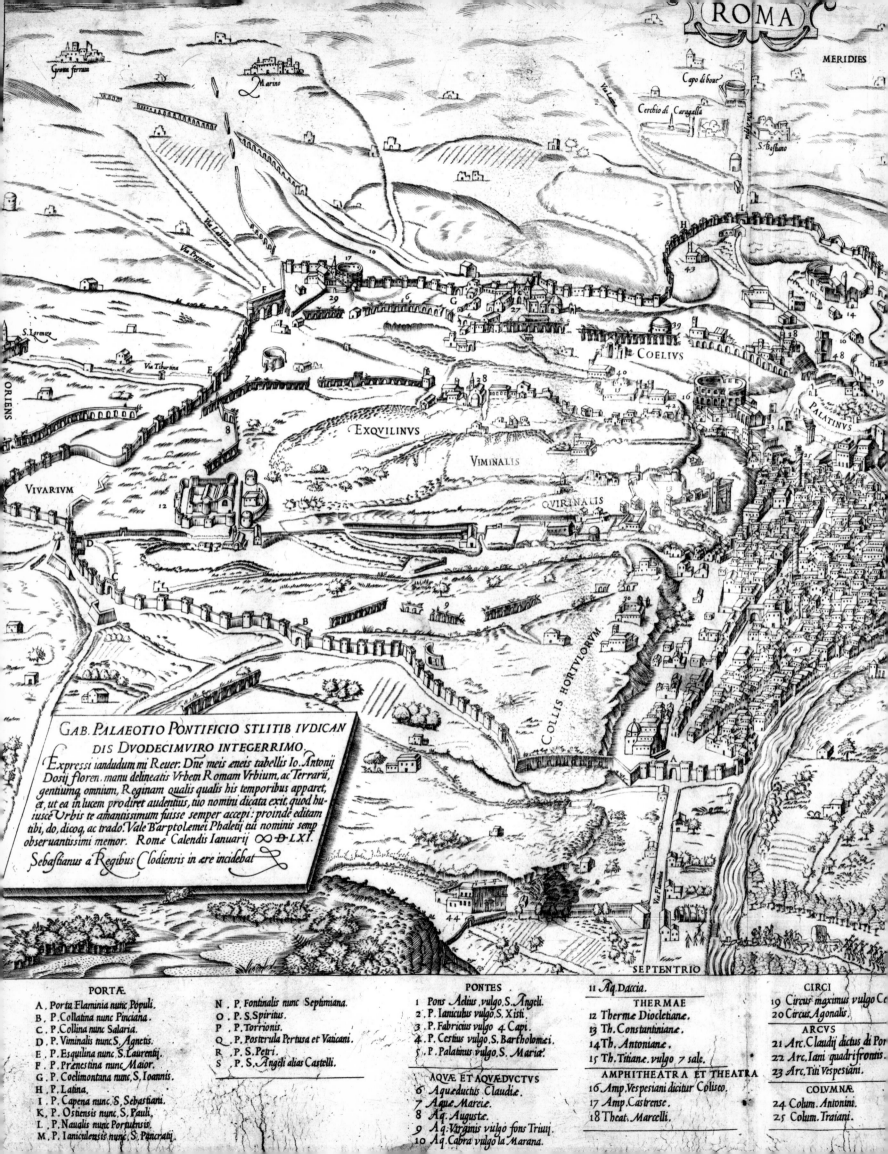

ROMA

MERIDIES

ORIENS

SEPTENTRIO

Groto ferrata
Marino
Capo di boue
Cerchio di Caragalla
S. Bastiano
S. Lorenzo
Via Labicana
Via Prenestina
Via Tiburtina
COELIVS
EXQVILINVS
VIMINALIS
QVIRINALIS
VIVARIVM
COLLIS HORTVLORVM
PALATINVS
Via Flaminia

GAB. PALAEOTIO PONTIFICIO STLITIB IVDICAN
DIS DVODECIMVIRO INTEGERRIMO.
Expressi iandudum mi Reuer: Dñe meis æneis tabellis Io. Antonij
Dosij floren. manu delineatis Vrbem Romam Vrbium, ac Terrarii,
gentiumq, omnium, Reginam qualis qualis his temporibus apparet,
et, ut ea in lucem prodiret audentius, tuo nomini dicata exit, quod hu-
iusce Vrbis te amantissimum fuisse semper accepi: proinde editam
tibi, do, dicoq, ac trado. Vale Barptolæmei Phaletij tui nominis semp
obseruantissimi memor. Romæ Calendis Ianuarij ∞ D LXI.
Sebastianus a Regibus Clodiensis in ære incidebat

PORTÆ

A. Porta Flaminia nunc Populi.
B. P. Collatina nunc Pinciana.
C. P. Collina nunc Salaria.
D. P. Viminalis nunc S. Agnetis.
E. P. Esquilina nunc S. Laurentij.
F. P. Prænestina nunc Maior.
G. P. Coelimontana nunc S. Ioannis.
H. P. Latina.
I. P. Capena nunc S. Sebastiani.
K. P. Ostiensis nunc S. Pauli.
L. P. Naualis nunc Portuensis.
M. P. Ianiculensis nunc S. Pancratij.
N. P. Fontinalis nunc Septimiana.
O. P. S. Spiritus.
P. P. Torrionis.
Q. P. Posterula Pertusa et Vaticani.
R. P. S. Petri.
S. P. S. Angeli alias Castelli.

PONTES

1 Pons Aelius, vulgo S. Angeli.
2 P. Ianiculus vulgo S. Xisti.
3 P. Fabricius vulgo 4 Capi.
4 P. Cestius vulgo S. Bartholomei.
5 P. Palatinus vulgo S. Mariæ.

AQVÆ ET AQVÆDVCTVS

6 Aqueductis Claudie.
7 Aque Marcie.
8 Aq. Auguste.
9 Aq. Virginis vulgo fons Triuij.
10 Aq. Cabra vulgo la Marana.
11 Aq. Daccia.

THERMAE

12 Thermæ Diocletiane.
13 Th. Constantiniane.
14 Th. Antoniane.
15 Th. Titiane, vulgo 7 sale.

AMPHITHEATRA ET THEATRA

16 Amp. Vespesiani dicitur Coliseo.
17 Amp. Castrense.
18 Theat. Marcelli.

CIRCI

19 Circus maximus vulgo C
20 Circus Agonalis.

ARCVS

21 Arc. Claudij dictus di Por
22 Arc. Iani quadrifrontis.
23 Arc. Titi Vespesiani.

COLVMNÆ

24 Colum. Antonini.
25 Colum. Traiani.

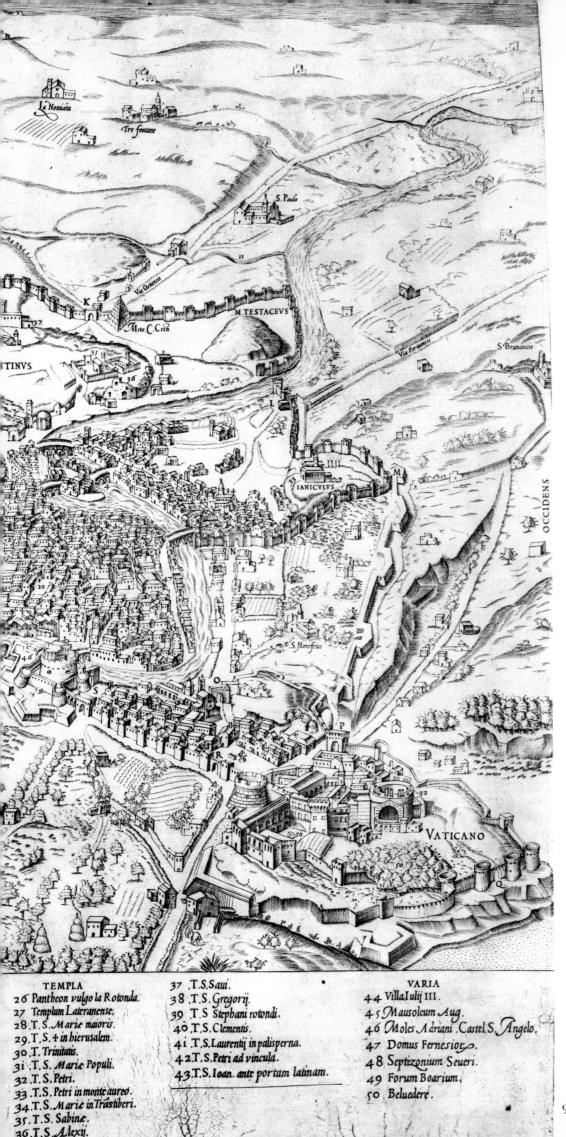

La Nonnata

Tre fontane

S. Paulo

Via Ostiensis

M. TESTACEVS

Mōte C. Cesú

Via Portuensis

S. Brancacio

TINVS

IANICVLVS

OCCIDENS

S. Honofrius

VATICANO

TEMPLA	37	T. S. Saui.	VARIA
26 Pantheon vulgo la Rotonda.	38	T. S. Gregorij.	44 Villa Iulij III.
27 Templum Lateranense.	39	T. S. Stephani rotondi.	45 Mausoleum Aug.
28 T. S. Marie maioris.	40	T. S. Clementis.	46 Moles Adriani. Castel. S. Angelo.
29 T. S. + in hierusalem.	41	T. S. Laurentij in palisperna.	47 Domus Fernesior.
30 T. Trinitatis.	42	T. S. Petri ad vincula.	48 Septizonium Seueri.
31 T. S. Marie Populi.	43	T. S. Ioan. ante portam latinam.	49 Forum Boarium.
32 T. S. Petri.			50 Beluedere.
33 T. S. Petri in monte aureo.			
34 T. S. Marie in Trastiberi.			
35 T. S. Sabine.			
36 T. S. Alexij.			

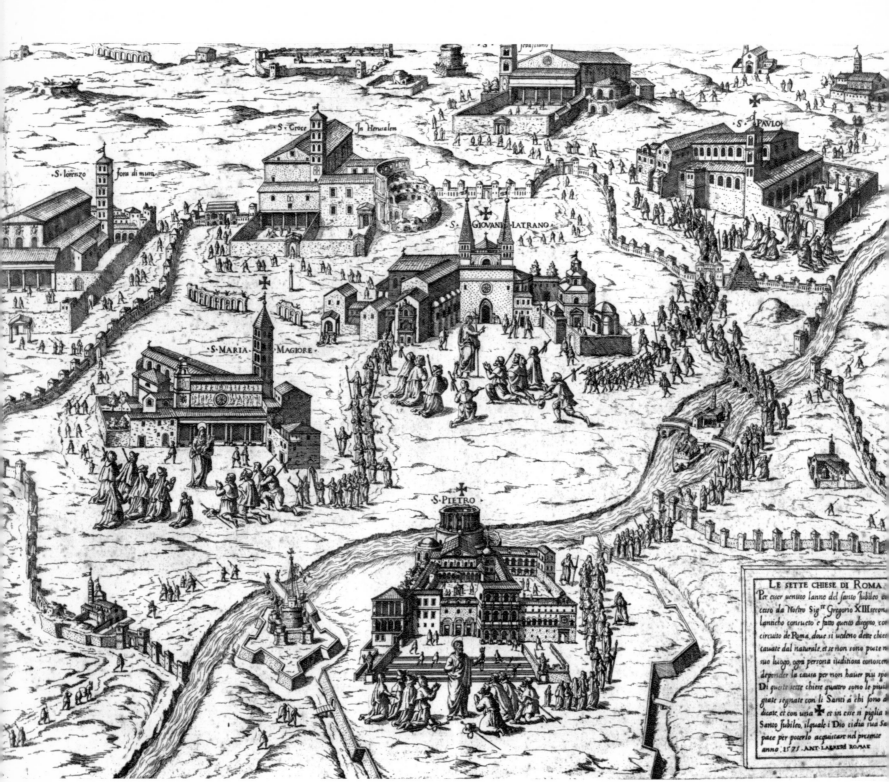

S·lorenzo fora di muni S·Croce In Herusalem S·GIOVANI·LATRANO S·PAVLO S·MARIA·MAGIORE S·PIETRO

LE SETTE CHIESE DI ROMA

95

night, and seven hundred public baths. Plants and fruits utterly foreign to Europe, such as peaches and pomegranates, were eaten by everybody while silk-making, hitherto a secret of the Chinese, was a flourishing industry. It is not surprising that Christians, finding themselves forced to live in such a place, became Muslims.

But for the most part, the relations between Christians and Muslims were a highly uncertain affair. To the Christian, the Muslim, however cultured, was the Abomination of Desolation who stood in the Holy Places. To the Muslim, the Christian worshipped a trinity of gods instead of one. Christian and Muslim did not necessarily fight. They might exchange blows, or books, and there was one place where the abomination met the polytheists and got on magnificently. This was Sicily.*

Sicily had been conquered by the Arabs of Kairouan, but it had been reconquered by the same Robert Guiscard who had lent aid to the enemies of Pope Gregory VII and then given him his dubious assistance. Guiscard was a free-booter, but subsequently the Christian rulers of Sicily were men of cultivation. Roger II was so impressed by his Muslim subjects that he readily adopted many of their ways, so much so that he was known to more conservative European Courts, including that of the Pope, as the "Sultan of Sicily." He wore Muslim clothes, he invited learned Muslims to his Court, he held free and frank discussions with them on religious matters, he encouraged the translation of Arabic works, and he even wore a robe which had a Kufic inscription embroidered on its hem. He had a chapel decorated with the same ornamental style of Arabic writing, and proudly boasted that one of the greatest geniuses of the Arab world, al-Idrisi, was at his Court. It was al-Idrisi who made the map of the world.

The crown of Sicily passed, in due course, to Frederick II who, as the Holy Roman Emperor, insisted that the inhabitants of his Holy Roman Empire learn from their Muslim betters. He founded a university at Naples and supplied it with a collection of Arabic works in translation. He sent to Bologna a translation of the works of Aristotle with a famous letter in praise of practical knowledge "without which," he said, "we cannot live this mortal life in freedom." The re-education of Europe which we, nowadays, call the Renaissance had begun.

The Renaissance had begun, but it had a long course to run before it

94 A view of Rome as it was in the 16th century, before Pope Sixtus V started his city-planning drive. The Esquiline, the Viminal and Quirinal Hills were at that time almost deserted. Sixtus V drove roads through the area and encouraged people to live there by remitting their taxes. The area of the Borghese Gardens, the Pincian Hill and the Spanish Steps were also without houses. As can be seen at the bottom right, the dome of St Peter's had not yet been started. This map by Antonio Dosio is in the Vatican Library.

95 A print (by Lafréry) of pilgrims making the circuit of the seven pilgrimage churches: St Peter's, St John Lateran, St Mary Major, St Paul Outside-the-Walls, St Sebastian, the Holy Cross and St Laurence Outside-the-Walls. The Christian practice of making this pilgrimage is known to have been well-established before the 8th century.

* See, for a fuller description, Amari's famous work *Storia dei Musulmani di Sicilia* or, in English, Hitti's *History of the Arabs*.

came to anything. First, the Romans turned it into grand opera. We have seen how the classical Romans built up a myth about themselves. This myth survived the centuries and generated in the mind of a barber's son, Cola di Rienzi, the idea of restoring the Senatus Populusque Romanus, with himself as Tribune of the People. Since the popes were away in Avignon, involved in a quarrel which I cannot here describe, he got his way with a vengeance. On August 15th 1347, he crowned himself with no less than six crowns and had his arms emblazoned with the keys of St Peter and the letters S.P.Q.R. Petrarch, the poet, who was also seized by a passion for the Roman myth, thought him a wonderful man. "What force," exclaimed the poet, "can stand against the name of Romans?" The answer was, as usual, the Romans themselves. Tiring of Rienzi's theatricalities and his complete inability to govern, they demanded his death. He was assassinated and his body was thrown into the Tiber.

Nobody else tried to rule in the magic name of classical Rome until our own times, when a journalist, Benito Mussolini, revived such ancient symbols as the *fasces*. He, too, in due course was assassinated for incompetence and his body (the Tiber not being handy) hung by the feet in a gasoline station.

But such men cannot be taken seriously as revivers of Rome. They were revivers of nonsense. In any case, the culture of Rome was essentially a Greek thing, as we have seen. Inevitably, then, it needed men who understood that language to bring about any true re-birth of classical studies. Back in the 9th century the Arabs had such men, but the Italians waited until the 15th century before they got hold of them, at least in sufficient numbers to awaken an interest beyond a narrow circle of studious scholars.

This happened in 1448, when the Emperor John Palaeologus came from Constantinople with his full Court to discuss re-union of the Church of Rome. The Pope had been expelled from Rome and was in Florence, so the Emperor met him there. Italian scholars were intensely curious to see real Greek philosophers, imagining them to be, as we do, men clad in flowing white with profound expressions and an immense store of wisdom.

This time the result was once again opera, but comic rather than grand. Greek philosophers had not changed very much from the time when they had descended *en masse* upon the intellectuals of Rome. They were vain, quarrelsome, frivolous in their opinions, shallow in their arguments and absurd in their appearance. They affected long beards, strange hats and they painted their eyebrows. They could,

96 *During the Renaissance and until the Counter-Reformation, Rome was celebrated for its immorality. Prostitution flourished and some courtesans made so much money that they were able to endow churches and be buried in them with honorific inscriptions. Married life was rendered precarious in many ways—husbands were not only unfaithful, they were often tempted to send their wives to join the ranks of the courtesans and to live off the proceeds in idleness. This portrait, of a baker's wife, is generally held to be a picture of the painter's mistress. It is by Raphael.*

97

however, speak Greek (of a sort) and they were listened to.

Here, once more, we have a moment of history which we feel should be dramatic. Italy, hungry for the knowledge of the Greeks, sits at the feet of their descendents. The wisdom of the ancients, distilled by the ages, is passed on. The torch of knowledge changes hands, spreading thereby a light in the darkness of Western Europe.

What did they really hear? Let me give an indication. The most prominent philosopher among the visiting Greeks was Giorgius Gemistus, who later called himself Gemistus Plethon. He had been born at Constantinople in 1355 and, as we might expect, he had found his education not among the Christians, but among the Muslims. As a young man he had gone to the Court at Adrianople, then a centre of Islamic power, and studied philosophy. When he came to Florence he was still handsome and had a beautiful speaking voice.

His principal notion was that everybody should abandon Christianity and take up a new religion, founded on Plato. He had made up the religion himself. There was a supreme god, Zeus, who gave birth to Ideas: these Ideas were called the god Poseidon, who was Logic, Atlas and Pluto who were Substance in its immortal state, Kronos and Aphrodite, who were substance in its decaying state, Dionysos, who was Motion ... and so on, in a long series of similar puerilities.

He had followers who called him "the mystagogue of sublime and celestial dogmas" (a fair enough name indeed), and who thought he was Plato re-incarnated.

It happens that a fragment of his work survives, which lets us know in his own words some of his opinions. In case the reader should wish to sit among the Florentines and visiting Romans on the bright morning of the world of learning, here, condensed, is what Gemistos thought about sex.

Since there is a chain of life extending from Zeus which must not be interrupted, "it is our duty, in the matter of having children, to leave the issue to the gods themselves, and as far as we are ourselves concerned to shoulder the duty incumbent upon us and render the service we owe to our common humanity and the whole universe; ... the provident design of Zeus for the continuance of the community between mortal and immortal beings, as that community appears in the shape of our human kind, must not be impeded by the abstinence of many from the pleasures of the senses ... man, in addition to his other duties, ought to be a citizen and not a solitary."

Reproduction of the species being a duty we owe to god, all sexual misconduct and sexual aberration must be punished. Those guilty of

97 *St Paul on the road to Damascus. A painting by Caravaggio which is in Santa Maria del Popolo. A man of immense talent and violent temperament, Caravaggio brought to Italian art a note of realism which offended many connoisseurs but brought him the protection of a cardinal. He was renowned for his fights, his pæderasty and his precocious mastery of the techniques of his art. He died aged forty-nine in Porto Ercole, having previously been driven out of Italy because he had murdered a young man.*

unnatural offenses "must be purified by fire: the offender and his accomplice must both be burned alive." This also is to be the punishment for adulterers, panders, pimps and anyone who rapes a woman. For good measure, he adds that anyone who disagrees with him should be burned alive, too. Evidence of good conduct might allow the condemned person to escape the stake, but only to suffer imprisonment for a term of years.*

While this brief specimen may not serve to show all that Gemistus Plethon thought in such matters, it does show that he could not have read much Plato.

But it did not matter if Gemistus Plethon was something of a charlatan and a windbag, he and his successors had set a fashion. More, it was a fashion which pleased princes and even popes. Antiquity became the hobby of rich men and prelates. Classical Rome had been dead: now it was found again, and, most importantly of all, it was considered respectable.

This was a revolutionary thing, especially for artists. The sources of inspiration for an artist of genuine talent are very rarely respectable and he spends a good deal of his time defending his conduct and his ideas, the roots of which he never really understands. But the marvel of the Renaissance was that, for the first time, an artist could look with his own eyes at the world about him and describe what he saw with his paint-brush or his chisel without blushing for what he had done. He had only to see that his work conformed in some way to the art of the Greeks and Romans, and all was well with popes and patrons. Thus Rome, which for some time had been on the periphery of events, came into its own again. It was littered with examples of sculpture and architecture of the past and it now became profitable to copy them, or adapt them to the artist's own needs.

The art and architecture of the Greeks had been a fine, but limited, achievement. The Romans had added nothing to it, but had so multiplied its examples by copying that, in spite of wholesale destruction, a vast museum of what the Greeks had done lay ready to hand. The artists of the Renaissance took their opportunity—but in their own way.

The Greeks, in the final phase of their art, had tied themselves up with rules. The Doric style, for one instance, grew so complicated in its apparent simplicity that it was dropped as too difficult. The Renaissance artists sometimes did not know and, in practice, never cared for

98 *Borromini was the architect of this church of St Ivo, which is dramatically set in the courtyard of the palace now housing the State Archives. With Borromini architecture became fluid, rippling and infinitely various in its aspects. More truly original than Bernini, Borromini lacked the other artist's discipline. Bernini continuously disparaged Borromini's work, and it is true that its fancifulness sometimes goes too far. But Borromini's buildings, seen in the Roman sunshine, are wonderfully successful essays in the play of light and shade.*

* For this and a fuller description of Gemistus Plethon's thought, see the documents in Ernest Barker's *Social and Political thought in Byzantium.*

99 *The most gifted man in the baroque era was Gian-Lorenzo Bernini, who dominated it, because of both his outstanding talents and his skill in keeping rival artists in the background. The Fountain of the Four Rivers in the Piazza Navona is an example of his imagination, skill and daring. It carries an obelisk high in the air on an arch of rusticated travertine. There are four giant statues, which represent the River Plate, the Danube, the Ganges and the Nile. The detail on the left is of the River Ganges, which was sculpted, after the design of Bernini, by Claude Poussin. The giant on the right represents the River Danube. It was also designed by Bernini, and it was executed by one of his most distinguished disciples, Antonio Raggi.*

100 *The baroque style was a revolt against the monotony and repetitiveness of the classical orders in architecture, and against the stiffness and dullness of the mannerists in sculpture. The variety and movement which was brought into buildings is well illustrated in this church, Santa Maria della Pace by Pietro da Cortona, one of the seminal geniuses of the baroque movement.*

these limiting rules. They, therefore, produced an art which, ostensibly based upon the classical models, would have shocked the ancients for its looseness, its vulgarity and its brashness. It was, however, the greatest achievement till then—and perhaps till now—in the history of our civilisation's struggle to create beautiful and permanent things. Italy had, at last, caught up with the Arabs. The rest of Europe had now to catch up with Italy. That is why in Rome, as the saying goes, things are always a hundred years earlier than you think. In the world of Islam, however, they are earlier by several centuries. Islam civilised us by its example. When we look at a beautiful thing for its own sake, when we seek to make ourselves cultured, when we enjoy the good and cultivated pleasures of life without self-condemnation and remorse, we should thank the Arabs. Perhaps that is why among certain sections of our society, such things are still regarded as exotic.

But the Renaissance was never a truly Roman thing. Rome borrowed it, as it had borrowed all its culture for centuries. Artists, writers and scholars came to Rome from all over Italy (and in particular from Florence and Naples), but they came because Rome had the money to pay them for their work. When they arrived, they were given jobs to do. The artists were set to beautifying palaces and churches: they created masterpieces, but the Romans never looked upon them as much more than highly skilled craftsmen. The scholars were given food, money and lodgings at the houses of the great, from the Pope downwards. They sat at rich men's tables, but they were expected to sing for their supper. Their position, unless they were very lucky, was that of menials whose duty it was to display their wit and their learning when their masters and betters, with their bellies full of food after dinner, were too lazy to make conversation for themselves. A scholar was shown off by a noble much as he showed off a prize dog or a fine horse. The scholars cost more than a dog, but not always more than a horse.*

For Rome was a city, not of artists and scholars, but of courtiers. There was the Papal Court itself, and around it a number of satellite courts, sometimes rivalling it in magnificence, maintained by cardinals, princes and the great families. The cultivated Roman of the Renaissance was far from the bold, enterprising, universally endowed man that romantic historians of the time would have us believe. A Frenchman, Joachim du Bellay, has left us a famous picture of how one had

* See Pio Pecchai's *Roma nel Cinquecento* (1957) in the series on the history of Rome published by the Istituto di Studi Romani for a corrective to the glorious-morning school of writing about the Italian Renaissance.

to behave to be thought a gentleman in Rome. "He must walk with a grave pace," says du Bellay, "smile gravely at every acquaintance, weigh each word, saying "Messer, yes" or "Messer, no" and from time to time injecting a "That's so" or "Sir, your servant." He must kiss gentlemen's hands like a gentleman, and hide his poverty under a bold manner." Penniless, servile, dependent on a master for his living, and a jackanapes—this was the typical Roman of the time that we have been taught to believe was so splendidly free.

With the Renaissance, Rome became immoral. So did the papacy. Nor should this surprise us. We have seen that the classical culture left people living under it without a certain guide to right and wrong. When it was revived, it loosened the restraints that Christianity had fastened upon its followers.

Historians who are enemies of the Church have seized upon the profligacy of the popes in this period, and rightly so. They have, perhaps, been too enthusiastic. Alexander VI, a Borgia, was too tempting to tell the whole truth about. Although he was a bad man, it is forgotten that he was a good pope, inasmuch as he was an able administrator of the Church. When he died, he was much respected, and so was the Borgia name. Lucrezia Borgia's crimes, along with her poison rings, would seem to be romantic inventions—there is, at any rate, no sound evidence for them. However, the Borgias of popular history, however highly coloured their story may be, do very well as examples of the morals of the Renaissance. They may not have done all the evil they are supposed to have committed, but if they didn't, others certainly did.

But let us leave these too-much-discussed people and turn to the streets of Rome. They were full of whores. So were the palaces, but there the whores were called courtesans, or in Italian *cortigiane,* that is to say, with no little irony, female courtiers. From these down to the lowest drabs (who were called whores "of the candle"), Roman life in the high Renaissance revolved round the illicit love affair.

It was by no means a picture of unrelieved squalor. There were very rich prostitutes, some of whom could afford to endow churches and be buried in them when they died. One such lay in peace in the church on top of the Spanish Steps until a more respectable age took away the tomb that she had worked and paid for.

But the profligacy of the Renaissance, which so fascinated our fathers and our grandfathers, was short-lived. Nor is it, to us, so very shocking. It does not strike us as either remarkable or unusually wicked that Benvenuto Cellini, as he tells us, lacking a suitable companion for

101 *Velasquez' portrait (1650) of Innocent X hangs in the Gallery of the Doria-Pamphili Palace, Innocent X being a member of the Pamphili family, to whose interests he was devoted. His papacy was marked by the fact that he allowed his affairs to be run by his sister, Donna Olympia, who interfered so much in ecclesiastical preferment that protests were raised in all parts of the Catholic world.*

102

103

a feast given to some prostitutes, dressed up a boy who was his lover as a woman and took him, with success, along. We know pretty much what the table conversation was like.

To us—to me, at any rate—it is more interesting that all this was suddenly and ruthlessly stopped. The Counter-Reformation made Rome moral, at least in outward appearances. This, in the writings of my predecessors, is always, I notice, spoken of with a note of melancholy. Yet, living in Rome, I have discovered that the repression gave rise to a burst of artistic activity as vigorous, if not as broad, as the Renaissance. It is the art that our grandfathers disliked so very much —the Baroque.

102 *Interior of the Doria Palace. This picture shows the Dutch Salon. It was decorated in the 18th century with pictures by Breughel the Elder and a superb Gobelin tapestry showing a winter scene in the Netherlands, executed for Louis XIV.*

103 *Again the Doria Palace, in this case its Venetian Salon, which is also 18th-century but decorated throughout by Venetian artists and artisans. The picture on the wall is of the school of Guardi.*

104 It was the custom in the 16th century for Roman nobles and the popes to celebrate great events with public entertainments on a magnificent scale. However, this tournament, given by Pius IV in 1565, was the last to be held in the Vatican. The sobering effects of the Council of Trent were beginning to make themselves felt: and with the next pontificate the worldly behaviour of the popes was gone for ever.

105 An 18th-century view of St Peter's at the moment when the Pope is blessing the crowd. He can be seen in the central window under a canopy.

106 The back façade of St Mary Major is much admired: usually more, in fact, than Ferdinand Fuga's front façade. This photograph shows the work of three distinguished architects: the right-hand section and the cupola were done by Flaminio Ponzio, and the centre, including the steps, and left portion were by Carlo Rainaldi. The cupola on the left is by Domenico Fontana. The 48 foot high obelisk in the left foreground is the twin of the obelisk in the Piazza Quirinale and once decorated the entrance of the Mausoleum of Augustus.

107 The Piazza di Spagna viewed from the Spanish Embassy to the Holy See. On the right are the well-known Spanish Steps, built between 1721 and 1725. The steps lead to the French church of Trinità dei Monti, which can be seen at the top right. Since the steps led up to a church in honour of the Trinity, the architects planned the ascent to stress the notion of three: three flights, three sections, etc.

108 Pope Benedict XIV arriving at St Mary Major. He is approaching the elaborate and elegant façade that was built between 1741 and 1743 by Ferdinand Fuga, one of the last of the baroque artists. The picture is by Pannini and hangs in the Quirinal Palace.

109 A view of the Piazza Navona by the 18th-century painter Pannini. It was and still is a passion of the Romans to make what is called the "passeggiata": that is to say, a walk or a drive to some part of the city or its environs. And they like these excursions to be as varied as possible. To meet this taste the Piazza Navona used to be flooded from time to time so that the gentry could drive through it in their carriages. The practice was stopped when the piazza paving was levelled. Now on warm summer evenings, the Romans drive round it in their small family cars. The Piazza Navona was Pope Innocent X's favourite square and he commissioned Rainaldi and Borromini to build the flanking church of S. Agnese, while it was for him that Bernini designed the fountains.

110 Here a French painter (Caron) attempts to reconcile the classical tradition and the taste of Counter-Reformation Rome in this imaginative setting. The subject is the legendary announcement by the Tiburtine Sybil to Augustus that the Son of God would be born during his reign.

104

105

108

109 ▷

110

111

112

PART FIVE

Swan song

1

111 *This fantastic high-baroque monument was, in fact, made of lath and plaster and did not outlive the day of its completion. Prince Colonna had it made for the Feast of St Peter and St Paul, as on that day he celebrated, with fireworks, his honorific duty of presenting the Pope with a white mule. The "festa" was held in 1752 in the piazza in front of the Colonna Palace, and this frivolous set-piece was in the centre of the fireworks display.*

112 *The famous Trevi Fountain. It is the aqueduct which brings the Aqua Virgine to Rome and is so called because the story goes that a girl showed Roman soldiers, who were thirsty, where the spring was. Agrippa, in 19 B.C., first brought this water to Rome. His aqueduct fell into disrepair and was restored by Nicholas V, and later by Sixtus IV. Urban VIII again kept it in operation and finally under Clement XII this monumental backdrop was made by Nicolò Salvi in 1762. It is said that he used an idea or design of Bernini. It is a superstition that those who wish to return to Rome should throw a coin over their shoulder into the water. This picture shows a pope, probably Clement XIII, visiting the fountain. Note the papal umbrella and Swiss Guards in the right foreground.*

113 *Detail of the Trevi Fountain.*

AFTER APPROXIMATELY FIFTEEN CENTURIES OF CONTINUOUS existence Rome, in the 1600's, at last produced an art of her own. That this art strikes a great number of sensitive people as vulgar should not surprise us. Classical Rome was never a refined place, in spite of the efforts of a few to make it so. After that, when classical Rome died, the city came under the influence and, for a long time, under the direct rule of priests: men, that is, who spend their lives dealing with human nature in the raw, and that, again, is far from a refining influence. Romans never had much liking for the elegant, and their taste has never been pure. They were, and are, eclectics.

The style which, at long last, was invented in Rome (though not by Roman artists) is called today the Baroque. It was not called anything when in the 17th century it burst upon Europe. It was simply described as the-astonishing-things-they-are-doing-in-Rome. For rather more than a century, Rome set the taste of the Western civilised world. Then, swiftly, the baroque style was condemned, ironically enough on the grounds that it was not Roman. A classical revival set in, and "baroque" became a word of contempt. To some people past their fifties, it still is. But the artists of the Baroque have been lucky. They have benefitted from our determination to be cultured. We are nowadays so afraid of being thought ignorant or Philistines that we admire everything. We are helped in this by art dealers, who see to it that every school gets its turn, and art critics, who help the dealers clear their inventories.

Baroque, then, fetches as good prices as any other style. But there are many people who do not admire it as readily as they do, for instance, the Renaissance manner. They have an uneasy feeling that sometime, somewhere, it was dreadfully bad taste to like Baroque, and we examine our taste these days with the same critical attention that people used to apply to their manners. The attack on Baroque, however, was a prejudice. I had best begin, then, by briefly telling how the prejudice arose. It can thus be cleared out of the way.

In the first place there was a group of people, mostly English, who were convinced that they knew the Almighty's taste in architecture. It was for the Gothic. It, therefore, followed that the only way to build a church was to give it spires and pointed arches. This led Pugin, an architect in the revived gothic style, to fall on his knees in the middle of St Peter's basilica. When asked what he was doing, he said he was thanking God because he had detected a crack in the dome. Or so it is said. The story will do, true or invented. The gothic revival was quirkish and many of its supporters were eccentric and show-offs. It need not detain us. Few people think nowadays that eye-strain during divine service brings them nearer to the Deity.

A more serious attack on the Baroque came from another quarter. As everybody knows, there are some people who are quite sure that they know why the Pyramid of Cheops was built. It was designed to foretell the history of the world. All one has to do is to measure the thing up with a foot-rule, do some sums, and history, past, present and future, is explained. The striking thing about these amiable crackpots is that if you throw doubt on their theory, however politely, they get very annoyed. Now there are certain people who have Pyramidal theories about artists. They have the key: they know all; and they are rude to people (like myself) who do not believe them. These people are sure that an artist is as much the product of his times as the daily newspaper. There is nothing mysterious or inexplicable in what he does. Given knowledge of his politics, his religion, his sexual tastes, the economy he lives in and so forth, his work is perfectly predictable.

One of the commonest ways of hiding invincible ignorance is always to be ready with an answer. These people do not know anything about the processes of artistic creation—nobody does—but they do not like to admit it. This would not matter much, save for the fact that they are opinionated. This means they think that what they like is good and what they don't is bad. They like their own politics, they like their own religion—or lack of it—and they like their own class prejudices. Now, when they find a situation in history in which the politics disgust them, the religion is offensive to them, and the wrong set is at the top, they are compelled by the Pyramidal principles to say that the art done at that time is bad.

Great art, of course, has arisen and flourished under every conceivable form of government and religion: artists have come from every class of society and been patronised as much by cads as by gentlemen. The Pyramidists know this: but they avoid the difficulty with an ingenious method. Should they come across art which ought to be bad, they examine it to find out what it is. Having made a list of its characteristics, they then announce that there is Good Art and Bad Art, the latter being defined by the list of characteristics of the type of creative work under their attack. This type of logical falsity is one of the most warming and satisfactory activities of the human mind. We all practise it at some time or another (during, for instance, political elections) and we always feel fine while we are doing it. All the same, we are cheating.

I shall now explain why the Pyramidists feel it necessary to cheat with the Baroque.

In the course of my excursions in Rome, I spent many hours—totalling, I fancy, several days—in St Peter's. There, after growing accustomed to the grandeur of the design, I noticed a curious detail. The basilica is decorated with vast pilasters. All of these have marble bases. Those round the apse, where the Pope and his cardinals sit, are marble all the way to the top. Those in the nave are not. They are a stucco imitation of marble. The reason for this, I discovered, is that the money for building St Peter's ran out, and the reason for that, in turn, was Martin Luther.

The initial work on St Peter's was largely financed by the sale of indulgences. We have seen that the papacy claimed the power to bind or loose from the penalties of sin. An indulgence—which is not a permit to be wicked—is just such a loosening. It is granted when the sinner is considered to have performed such acts as warrant the belief that he has repented his sins and wishes to live in future according to the dictates of his religion. Thus a man who makes a discommoding pilgrimage, prays at certain altars, confesses his sins, hears Mass and takes the Sacrament, may reasonably be thought to be a man who takes his faith seriously. He may gain an indulgence. But since his act of confession has absolved him already, this indulgence is, so to speak, a religious profit. He can apply it, provided he prays, to souls in purgatory. *His* faith shortens *their* punishment. Should this seem strange, it should be remembered that although the basis of the Christian faith is the individual's responsibility towards God, its structure is that of a corporate organisation. Every Christian is a part of the body of the faith, both when living and when dead.

An indulgence, then, is a perfectly proper thing granted the tenets of Catholicism, and so far from encouraging slackness in morals, it insists on religious exercises. All is well with the system provided the morals of the priesthood, and especially the papacy, are fully Christian.

But in the Renaissance, they were not. The fashion for paganism helped to weaken the moral fibre of ecclesiastics, and especially in Rome. I do not say that if the papal court had refrained from collecting Roman statuary and manuscripts of the classics, it would have been pure. It had been corrupt at certain times in the past when its sins were only matched by its ignorance. But the Renaissance spread a glow round wrong-doing. Classical equivocation over morals, its lack of a fixed viewpoint, took the urgency out of living a holy life: and, for a priest, holiness must be urgent.

The result of this was that indulgences were sold for money. Cash had been taken from penitents for centuries. There is, after all, no other way of making bad conduct unattractive, short of prison or the whip. But now indulgences began to be sold with a certain cynicism: less attention was paid to the state of the penitent's soul, and more to the size of the price that could be got out of him. Something of the same sort can be found in many fund-raising organisations today. The object of the charity is often forgotten in the enthusiasm of extracting the cash.

Martin Luther, a dedicated theologian, who would have been more at home in the Middle Ages than his own times, saw how this and many other abuses could not be fitted into the closely-reasoned structure of Christianity. For a while Rome, open-minded and un-fanatical because of the mental atmosphere of the age, did not take him seriously. When it had permanently lost a vast number of Christian believers to him and his followers, it called a Council at Trent, which brought back reason to the Catholic Church and, in fact, did many of the things that Luther advised the Church to do. But it should be noted that it also deliberately stressed many aspects of the Catholic faith that Protestants disliked. It did not widen the Church. It reform-ed, and it narrowed.

This period of history is known as the Counter-Reformation. The Catholic faith became stricter, religious fervour was encouraged, immorality was not condoned, church-going was insisted upon and the Christian virtues once more triumphed in Rome over the pagan. In a word, there was an enforced religious revival.

To some people, a religious revival is a very repulsive affair. A Christian revival is particularly so for people who value the arts, for as we have seen the Christian faith is unhelpful towards such things. For the people who are sure they know what art is all about and where it comes from, the Counter-Reformation is a cultural disaster. It suppressed the spirit of the Renaissance and supplanted it with Christ-ian orthodoxy. It was obviously the death of great art.

114, 115 *Two examples of the innumerable canvases turned out as souvenirs for people who, in the 18th century, made the Grand Tour, which was obligatory for any educated gentleman. The first shows a view of the Forum from the Capitoline Hill and is painted by the Dutchman, Gaspard van Wittel. The second was painted by an Englishman, Archibald Skirving, in 1792, and shows some of his compatriots posing against a background of the Colosseum and the Arch of Constantine. The Grand Tour was very expensive, and Rome was one of the costliest stops on it.*

117

118

But it wasn't. Rome, flung upon itself, produced a splendid flowering. Under the Counter-Reformation, it turned itself into what is still the most beautiful city in the world. It is a baroque city. Naturally, therefore, the Pyramidists of art history had no alternative but to study the Baroque, observe its principles and to declare them the canons of bad art. That Rome was and is, undeniably, a lovely city did not deter them at all. They came each winter, enjoyed its beauty and went home and condemned it. In books and journals for more than a century, priests as patrons of art were reviled.

2

BUT ROME IS BEAUTIFUL, AND THOSE WHO ATTACK THE BAROQUE never, so far as I have read them, dare to deny it. Nor can anyone deny that it was the priests, that is the popes and cardinals, who ordered that Rome be made a handsome city and who paid the bill. A great deal of classical Rome remains, but it is grievously shattered, and stripped of everything that once made it a pleasure to the eye. The attempt to dig up more of it has made matters worse. Rome, like Athens, has its archaeological slums. As for the Middle Ages, there are a few towers, some churches, such as St Mary in Cosmedin, and a corner or two that take the eye and please the spirit—none more than the piazza and the arches of the church of St John and St Paul. But the Renaissance detested the Middle Ages and did away with its evidence whenever it could. Little of it is left in Rome. Rome cannot compare with a dozen other Italian towns that still, like San Gimignano, to the visitors' astonishment, are medieval from gate to gate. As for the Renaissance, Rome has great masterpieces, such as the Papal Chancellery, to show. But one does not live among the Renaissance. The core of Rome's astonishing beauty is in the long perspectives that open up everywhere in the old city, its ebullient statues splashing themselves with sunshine, its façades that leap and plunge like a school of dolphins. This is Rome: and this is the Rome the Counter-Reformation made. There is no denying it. The papal arms proclaim it from every wall: and, for those who cannot decipher them, there are the inescapable dates in the guide-book.

The art of the Baroque in Rome can best be enjoyed if it is approached in the spirit in which it was created—that is to say, in a worldly fashion. It is true that the theme of baroque sculpture and decoration is often—though not always—religious. But the popes did not spend the large sum of money which it cost in order to teach their subjects (for they were the rulers of Rome) to be better Christians. Popes, who are

116 *A portmanteau souvenir picture by Pannini, an 18th-century artist who specialized in such works and made a living by painting them. The picture is of an imaginary art gallery, and Michelangelo's Moses and Bernini's David and his Apollo and Daphne have been thrown in for good measure.*

117 *The French ambassador, Cardinal de Polignac, erected these monuments of lath and plaster and papier-maché to celebrate the birth of a son to the king of France in 1729. There was considerable rivalry among ambassadors and other men with money at their disposal in erecting these ephemeral displays. The artists of the time were, and had to be, virtuosi in designing them for their patrons.*

118 *Prince Camillo Rospigliosi gives a party for his peasants to celebrate the grape-harvest. Rome Museum.*

rarely fools about religious matters, were fully aware that the sort of art which does this best is the one that turns out plaster images. Before such things as these the faithful can concentrate their thoughts, not on the beauty of the object before them, but on the person that it summarily represents. They knew that one good preacher inside a church was a greater impulse to holy living than twenty stone saints on the façade. When one of them paid out good money for Bernini to build a fountain showing the four great rivers of the world supporting an Egyptian obelisk, it is unlikely that he considered its purpose was to support the Church's missionary effort. And when Pope Alexander VII commanded that the chair of St Peter be enshrined in a sunburst, supported by angels and four huge gesticulating figures of the Doctors of the Church, one may assume that he knew that Christianity had managed for centuries to get along without any such artistic bravura.

But, as I have described earlier in this essay, my excursions in Rome had taught me that the papacy cannot be understood unless it is remembered that, beside its all-embracing spiritual claims, it is also a monarchy, the supreme monarchy if other rulers could be persuaded to yield to it, and even when they cannot, a monarchy still.

After Martin Luther and the Protestant secession, the temporal claims of the papacy were denied by a large number of Christians, and questioned everywhere. Even at home, in their own Papal States, the papacy had a bedraggled look. Clement VII had been shut up by foreign troops in the Castel Sant'Angelo, and derided by drunken soldiers under his own windows. He had sold his jewels and even, symbolically enough, had Benvenuto Cellini melt down his tiaras. Cellini was accused of stealing gold from the sacred emblems. He denied so sacrilegious a crime. But it was clear that his accusers thought he was guilty, and were unable to see why he should not have been. It had become the policy to loot the Vatican of the movable personal property of the pontiff as he lay dying, even if he had been a very strong pope. With the papacy weakened, insulted and imprisoned, there was little reason why the pontiff should not be robbed while he was still alive.

The Sack of Rome (1527), when these events took place, is usually considered to mark the end of the Renaissance way of life in Rome and the beginning of a new one. From the point of view from which this essay is written it is interesting to note that the horrors and brutalities of the Sack were the product of a pure invention based upon a piece of fiction. The popes had claimed to make kings and, as we have seen, they based their right on the Donation. Now the troops of the Holy

Roman Emperor rode round the Pope's castle, sitting on mules, dressed up in papal vestments and singing ribald songs about the papacy. Later, the Holy Roman Emperor, Charles V, professed himself sorry that it happened and was not at all sure where the orders had come from. But it will be remembered that the papacy had invented the Empire in order to have the support of the Emperor's troops. Whatever the doubts might be as to who had ordered the bestialities and vandalism of the Sack of Rome, there was no doubt at all as to the sort of help that the papacy might henceforward expect from the imperial troops.

The Council of Trent reformed the church and gave back in full to the popes the spiritual authority which they had in part lost, because of the corruption they had permitted. The popes were once more revered: it remained for them to be admired. They were once again pastors: they had to show that they were still princes.

Nothing is more princely or less open to criticism than to embellish a city. The Council of Trent had made it certain that the papacy would grow in virtue (it was remarked, significantly, of Alexander VII that he was chaste) but a pope proclaiming and proving that he is virtuous would not make a striking impression on anybody but the most cynical observer. In any case, religious zeal had been taken care of by the Jesuits, who were sworn to be fervent in faith, even if the Pope was, by chance, not. They were the spiritual troops of the papacy, devoted with equal tenacity to obeying the Pope and getting their own way. With the Jesuits' increasing power and improving skills, it became clear that, on the purely religious side, the papacy of the Counter-Reformation was safe. The popes would either be good Christians or be made to appear so. The scandals of the Renaissance were made impossible, and have been ever since. The popes could safely embark upon temporal display.

It happened that at this juncture there arose an artistic genius. I know as much about the origins of genius as anybody, which is nothing at all. I therefore cannot say that the need of the popes produced Bernini, or whether Bernini would have flourished without it. Urban VIII said all there is to say upon the matter when he told Bernini that the artist was lucky to have him as pope, and that he was luckier to have Bernini alive during his pontificate. Rome, we may add, was lucky to have both of them.

3

I HAVE NO DOUBT THAT AS THE PREJUDICE AGAINST THE BAROQUE dies and the beauty of Counter-Reformation Rome becomes known to everybody, Bernini will be much written about. He will be ranked among the Great Artists, and we all know what they are like. They are temperamental, sexually naughty, rebels against society, despisers of money, embittered, devoted to their art, which at one stage of their career they would have given up were it not for the love of a good woman. Fortunately, there is still time to tell the truth about Bernini, without offence. He was a very great artist, and a very dull man. He was business-like, sociable, well-pleased with himself, married, and had only one mistress, whom he gave up when she took up too much of his time.

Gian-Lorenzo Bernini (1598–1680) was the son of a sculptor who, though not a very good one, was among the few of his time. They were not fat times for the arts. Such creative spirits as there existed were given too much to enthusiasm for their predecessors, and that is a bad thing for an artist. He may rejoice without bounds in his own work, but he should not be excessively impressed by anybody else's. He should like the great, provided they have been a long time dead, but only in order to improve on them. Nothing should awe him, except his own talent. The painters and sculptors of the Renaissance were men of this stamp. But unfortunately the abilities of Raphael and Michelangelo were such that when they were dead, it was thought even by artists that no-one could do better than they. There was nothing for it but to imitate them.

In the case of Michelangelo that had, unfortunately, already been done. In his later life, Michelangelo began to imitate himself, as may be seen clearly in the illustrations of this book (see plates 75-77). These imitations were the most renowned specimens of his art (he, himself, being then at the height of his fame) and they were the most copied. A copy brings out the weaknesses both of the model and the artist who is copying it. Thus it was with the followers of Michelangelo.

The master had drawn his inspiration from studying young men in their earliest manhood, a time of spectacular vigour in the lives of Italians everywhere, but especially in the northern cities such as Rome and Florence. The élan of Michelangelo's poses, the flash of eye, the rippling loveliness of the bodies he drew and carved had a basis in reality. His figures were heroic, but then Italian young men are, in fact, heroes, if only to themselves. Michelangelo's representation of them was so successful that he was able to use them for every figure he needed. His old men were young men with beards, his women young men with such attributes of femininity as he could fit into the heroic mould. But as age dimmed his sight, or his desires, he relied less upon

119 *This picture commemorates the visit in 1744 of King Carlo III of Naples to Pope Benedict XIV at the Quirinal Palace. The Quirinal Palace was started in 1574 as a summer palace for the popes and it was used by them until 1870, the time of the Risorgimento, when it became the official residence of the Chief of the Italian State. Painted by G. P. Pannini, this picture is in the National Museum of Capodimente, Naples.*

120 *Here Carlo III, on horseback, arrives at St Peter's. The reason for his visit to Rome was the celebration of his troops' victory over the Austrians at Velletri (just outside Rome) in 1744. Architecturally, the view in 1744 was precisely the same as it is today. Also by Pannini.*

119

120

121

121 *Until 1644 St Peter's was mostly bare of decoration and with white stuccoed walls. In that year Bernini, with forty of his own sculptors and craftsmen, started covering the walls and pillars with coloured marble, putti, armorial bearings, gold leaf and statues: it took him eight years. He had previously built the immense "baldacchino" which can be seen under the dome, and which covers the place where St Peter was buried. In the apse is the Chapel of the Chair of St Peter, which has a most spectacular altar-piece: this is also by Bernini. The last picture in this book is a detail photograph of it, and it can also be seen in colour in Plate 147. Inside the dome the words TU ES PETRUS are written in letters five feet high and in mosaic. Beneath the dome are four gigantic statues, each with a balcony above it. The one that can be seen is of St Helen, the mother of Constantine, who brought the wood and the nails of the Cross from Jerusalem.*

122 *A statue by the sculptor Canova. He was the leader of the reaction against the Baroque. Returning to what he conceived to be the classical Greek and Roman style, he was profoundly admired during his life, but his reputation sank immediately he was dead and it has never recovered. Here Paolina Borghese is shown as the Conquering Venus. Since she had to pose partially nude, and since she was the sister of Napoleon Bonaparte and the wife of Prince Camillo Borghese, the statue caused a scandal. When she was asked how she, a lady, could pose naked for an artist, she replied, "Ma la stanza era ben riscaldata" (that is to say, "But the room was well warmed") a phrase echoed in our own times by another celebrated woman, Miss Marilyn Monroe, who said that she had the central heating on. There is nothing new under the sun.*

nature to impress him and more upon his formidable skills. *David* strikes us as the statue of a person who might have lived: the figures in the Last Judgment, tremendous as they are in their effect, do not persuade us that they have ever existed apart from the wall of the Sistine Chapel. It was this phase of Michelangelo which dominated art after his death and, because it enshrined the cooling passions of an old man, the art of that time was cold. The leader of this chilly school was Bernini's father.

Gian-Lorenzo Bernini learned from him, but soon surpassed him. Having done so, he neither quarrelled with his father, nor pitied him, nor ran away from home. He was merely a dutiful and modest son, who thought and said that his father was the greatest sculptor of his age. He listened to his father's advice until the old man's death. He did not take it, but he always intended to do so. He was inventing, year by year, a whole new school of sculpture, but he had no notion that he was doing it. His aim was simply to be as good a sculptor as his father.

He had other models as well. These were the statues that were constantly being discovered in the ruins of classical Rome and which, by his time, had been gathered together in collections in which Bernini studied constantly.

I have made several excursions to the same collections, or at least to see those pieces which Bernini must have seen (for the collections have been much changed around). I could not see them with Bernini's eye: I am not a sculptor. But I could make some attempt to share his feelings. Scattered in various museums are pieces by Bernini that he made when he was still a boy. Now, looking at his early work and comparing it with the classical statues that he must have seen, it is clear that even as a boy, Bernini had more skill with the chisel. He could already do as much and more than any of the sculptors he studied. His designs may have been, at that early age, less strong. His technique was certainly more varied.

This should cause no surprise. Almost all the statues that were dug up or found at this time were copies. As we have seen, the Romans had no original art. As for the Greek originals, they were lost, or in Greece, which was as bad, since Greece was under the domination of the Turks and a dangerous place for an artist to travel in. Besides, what little Greek sculpture we have was mostly discovered since Bernini's time. The Greeks, in their subtleties with a chisel, surpassed Bernini, as they surpass everybody who came after them. But the Roman copies are mostly indifferently made. Lesser artists than Bernini might regard them with awe. But Bernini could scarcely have been deceived. At any rate, he returned to his father's studio and carved so much better than his classical forebears that he was instantly marked down as a genius—an artist, that is, who could serve in the glorification of the Pope.

But Bernini did not merely carve better than the Romans. He also thought better. There was, as we have seen, great need for a new idea, and Bernini supplied it. The classical sculptures had all stopped at the surface of the marble. The design, that is, was self-contained. It was all in the stance and the relation of the planes that the sculptor's chisel created. Bernini extended the design to include the space in which the statue stood. The composition leapt out of the marble and moulded the circumambient air.

Michelangelo's *David*, for example, is in repose. That of Bernini moves in a violent action and, as we follow the lines of it out and beyond the statue, we see that he has created in our mind's eye a shadowy, insubstantial Goliath. The bust of a Roman emperor gazes nobly into vacancy. The bust of a cardinal by Bernini creates, by the turn of its head, the darting of its glance, a group of listeners standing around it. Michelangelo's drapery hangs in magnificent monumental folds, or, with his followers, as a stiff drape tying down the figure. Bernini's drapery swirls out with the figure's movement in space. His statues are moving about. In fact, in one instance, when his subject was Louis XIV, Bernini told him to walk about and not to pose. The Sun King obeyed.

I have put Bernini's original invention in the way that he liked himself. His rivals described his style in less complimentary ways. Why, they asked, are all of Bernini's figures caught in a gale of wind? That is unkind, but it is also praise, however reluctant. To carve figures, in marble, that are blown upon by the wind, means that Bernini could, in a way, carve the air itself. And that is what he intended to do.

It was an authentic revolution. The wind that played round Bernini's statues blew away the classical rules of composition that had confused all but the most exceptional imaginations for a millennium and a half. It played throughout Rome in churches, on façades, round towers, and it blew through the paintings of the time, and never to more effect than when it swirled round the draperies of the figures that began to decorate the ceilings of temples and palaces.

It was perhaps a pity that Bernini was so clever. He painted and sculpted, but he also designed, and particularly for the theatre. He was a man of a certain theatricality himself. He enjoyed creating an effect. On one occasion he displayed a portrait-bust to the Cardinal

123 *This is an Englishman's view of the firework display given in honour of the election of Pope Pius VI. Wright of Derby was the painter, and though the show was undoubtedly very fine, it is improbable that Trajan's Column, the Pantheon and the Castel Sant'Angelo also left their usual sites to come to see it, too. These three monuments are in the middle distance left.*

123

124

Borghese, who was delighted with it. When the Cardinal finished his praises, Bernini, moving him round the statue, pointed out dolorously that the marble had cracked during the carving. He allowed just sufficient time for the Cardinal's bitter disappointment to be plain. Then he whisked away the cover from a second bust, a copy of the first, but perfect. He had, he explained, done it in one night. It is more probable that he took two weeks, as his contemporaries believed. But the *coup de théâtre* was not lessened by that.

When the great fountain of the Four Rivers in Piazza Navona was finished, Pope Innocent X, at Bernini's invitation, came to see it. Once again, Bernini was cast down. The sculpture was complete but, alas, there was no water and the jets were the essence of the design. As the pope turned away with a mixture of irritation and disappointment, Bernini made a signal. Water gushed from every orifice. It was childish but then, as every creative artist knows, so are patrons. A few tricks make the millionaire, the Foundation, the publisher or the editor feel that he is getting his money's worth: and Bernini, who died rich, knew a great deal about money.

No design of Bernini for the theatre has survived. But those of his imitators do. They are very baroque. It has, therefore, been said, and still is, that the Baroque, which owed so much to Bernini, is theatrical. In this way, it is thought that the baroque is explained. Nothing, in fact, is explained at all. Bernini certainly designed baroque stage settings: but he had already originated the style.*

4

WHILE BERNINI LIVED, ROME HAD BEEN IMITATED BY ALL EUROPE. When he died, dullness set in, baroque inspiration sputtered a while and then went out. An age of pettiness and small men began. Whenever, in European history, people have run out of ideas, they have fallen back on the argument that Greece and Rome had all the ones that were any good. So it was in the 18th century among the principal artists of Italy. Led by a competent nobody, Canova, the sculpture of the classical times was revived. Once more it was set up as the standard, and the limit, of artistic achievement. Stark white nudes, insipidly posed, were carved, exhibited and volubly admired by everyone who had any claim to be thought a person of taste. The whiteness was considered

124 *By the 19th century, tourists' notions of Rome had grown more sentimental, in keeping with the temper of the times. What W. S. Gilbert described as "the fascination frantic For a ruin that's romantic," was felt by every visitor. Here Samuel Palmer shows us how people saw Tivoli round about 1838.*

* Francesco Mochi and Stefano Maderno may have preceded him by a few years in the seminal ideas. Neither Bernini nor his contemporaries, however, were in any doubt as to who was really responsible for it.

199

particularly fetching. It echoed, it was said, the classic purity of ancient Rome.

One of the last of my excursions took me among these pallid examples of stone masonry. Though my curiosity could not really be roused by such work, it occurred to me to ask just how near they were to the Roman taste: not the Roman taste of the classical myth, but the thing the Romans really liked. I went back to the collections and there I saw something that I might have expected. On many of the statues, especially those found recently, were traces of paint.

The truth is that Greek and Roman statues were never white.* They appear so because they have been cleaned by sun and rain. When they were new, they were painted. The colours were purple, yellow, violet, blue, red and brown. The eyes of the statues were painted to resemble living eyes, the drapery was naturalistically coloured, the parts supposed to be naked flesh were tastefully tinted, probably a dull red, and every statue had painted hair.

That was how it really was, but the myth of Rome, once more prevailing, was now so strong that its devotees could afford to ignore the facts. Rome became the centre of a foreign cult. Foreign artists from all over Europe, led (and exhorted) by Goethe, came to live in Rome. The Romans themselves ignored them, as indeed they ignored everything but the opera, gossip, trips out of town and the carnival. The impulse of the Counter-Reformation being exhausted, even religion fell into decay. Pope Pius VII, when asked to restore some of the Holy Week ceremonies that had been allowed to fall into desuetude, replied, "Why not? It will amuse the English." By the beginning of the 19th century, the foreign enthusiasts, the foreign visitors, had in truth taken over such life as was left in the enervated city. The myth was triumphant.

At this point my researches stopped. Rome, from now on, was a museum city, and such I thought it to be today. But there was a final irony left for me. I, who had spent so long a time in deploring the blindness of others to plain facts, was ignoring something which was underneath my own nose. Let me, in an epilogue, explain.

* The evidence, together with a long quotation, is to be found in Richter's *The Sculpture and Sculptors of the Greeks* (1929).

PART SIX *New Rome: a personal report*

1

THAT WAS THE LAST OF MY EXCURSIONS INTO HISTORY. I HAD confirmed, as Pope Pacelli had said, that most of what we call history cannot be believed, and I had decided that what is true cannot really be liked. So I let the dead past bury its dead. I left Rome and I looked about me at the world today. Instead of the past I studied the present. I visited a dozen other cities, some in Europe, some in America, two in Africa. I admired sky-scrapers in Cairo, roads in New York and machinery in Milan.

I was refreshed. But when I came back to Rome I was shut in the past again and it did not occur to me, at first, that I could escape.

But in the end I did. I made the last of my Roman investigations. Once more, then, I ask you to accompany me to find the answer to a question, but this time we shall study not monuments, but people, and I shall do my best to make them live before you. I shall quote their words, as I heard them, and I shall describe their manner of life.

This is the question to which I found an answer. I had always taken it for granted, like the rest of the world, that a citizen of Rome must be profoundly affected by the weight of the tradition behind him, the sight of the past lying all about him, and the sense of being a citizen of the Eternal City. But *is* he?

The answer is surprising. It is not the Caesars or the Pontiffs who have shaped Rome today. It is Henry Ford. This is how I discovered it.

I had grown accustomed to being wakened each morning by the bells of S. Lorenzo in Lucina. Then, one day, shortly after I had returned from a visit to New York, I was wakened a little earlier. It was still dark. The bells had not yet begun to ring. But an errand-boy was walking down the street, whistling. The tune was catching: but it did not sound very Italian. Besides, the boy had not yet learned it properly. The next morning, he was better at it. The next, better still. On the third morning, he walked down my antique street whistling the tune without a mistake from beginning to end and so could I. It was a bouncing, fresh little tune that raised my spirits.

He whistled it every morning for the next week, and I would lie in bed looking at the dark shapes of the palaces through my windows and whistling with him. I grew very fond of the melody. It reminded me of the fresh, bright things I had seen on my travels in the world of today. Then, one morning, he did not come, nor the next, nor the next. I waited for him, hoping to hear him with an intensity that surprised me. He never came again. It was left to bells once more to wake me, and they rang, for me, very drearily. I would get up, open the window, and glower at the palaces on either side of the street. Living in the past, I was seized by a profound nostalgia for the present. Next day a card came inviting me to be present at the celebration of the 2711th anniversary of the foundation of the city. It was my duty to go, and I went.

The audience was made up of civilised, cultured Romans, all with a deep sense of history, since they were members of learned historical societies. The celebration was held in a place sacred with memories, the Capitoline Hill. Ambassadors, prelates, scholars and men with ancient names were there, surrounded by gorgeously uniformed retainers. We sat in a great painted hall in the Palace of the Conservators. We had been ushered up purple carpeted steps by footmen in historic livery. We were the élite. Everything led me to expect a most impressive morning. In fact the ceremony turned out to be a dismal failure. I am told that it always is.

The Mayor of Rome was in the chair, the latest representative of the Caesars. Perhaps he was, after all, not so bad a representative. Some of the Caesars ran to fat; some of them made chaffing speeches; and many, I imagine, scratched their rumps while listening to orators. Some, too, I'm sure, made a glorious muddle of a great occasion. This one made the worst I have ever seen.

Rome gives prizes to scholars each year for essays on history, for bibliographical studies, and for essays in classical Latin. As he gave away the awards, the Mayor dropped the illuminated scrolls, grabbed silver wolves by their hindquarters, got names backwards. Then he awarded the prize for Latin. "It has been won," he said, "by Father ..." He stopped. He squinted at the list in his hands. A Jesuit priest, smiling nervously, got up from my row and went forward. "By Father ..." said the descendant of the Caesars. He looked up at us. "On the list it just says 'Father' ... and then blank," he complained. Father Blank hesitated in the aisle, blushed, and swallowed heavily. The rest of us tittered. "Well," said the Mayor, a man of action down to his last straining waistcoat button, "well, let's say it was awarded to a Father.

125 *A magnificent example, by Ingres, of the type of portrait which could be seen all over Europe in the houses of people aiming to be considered cultured. In this picture, which is of François-Marius Granet, a painter, the Quirinal is shown in the background. In others there are pieces of sculpture, ruins or Roman landscape. The fashion for such things was started by Goethe. Tradition has it that Granet, best known for his landscape work, was allowed by Ingres to paint in his own background.*

125

Come forward, Father whoever-you-are. My congratulations." Father whoever-he-was tripped over his soutane, accepted a document and enjoyed what the Mayor had left him of a moment of glory for which he may have studied and composed for twenty years. Father whoever-he-was returned to his seat, red in the face, with our chuckles in his ears.

We were not cruel. We were bored. We had listened to a scholar telling us at length that Rome had been the tutor to the world. Another had described how proud he was to be a Roman and the Mayor had described how proud he was to be a mayor. We were grateful for a touch of life in a dead morning.

I left before the ceremony ended. I walked down the empurpled stairs, past the liveried footmen, out into the fresh air. I sat on the steps of the Church of the Ara Coeli and looked out over the ruins of the Forum. I remembered that the historian Edward Gibbon had sat on these steps, looked at the same panorama and made up his mind to write the history of Rome's decline and fall. I reflected that he must have been in the same mood as I was, for in his view history was little but the record of the crimes and follies of mankind. I thought that he might have added that the crimes and follies are monotonously alike.

That evening I was a guest at an entertainment. As I was being introduced, I noticed a man whom I had seen at the morning's celebration on the Capitoline Hill, and there was a vacant chair beside him. When my hostess released me I made for the chair. I said:

"Professor, I saw you this morning..."

"At the ceremony, yes," he said. "You were looking bored."

He was, I suppose, about forty, slender-faced, with beautiful hands. His Italian was Roman; that is to say, he spoke with the most musical language in the world, for the Roman prides himself on the lilt of his dialect and to keep it he will cheerfully murder the grammar of the language. I was aware that to his ear my Italian, as a foreigner, would sound like the grinding of a cement-mixer. In as musical a tone as I could muster, I said:

"I was trying to concentrate on the grandeur of your eternal city. I didn't succeed very well."

"For three hours?" he said. "What a lesson you foreigners are to us flighty Italians. I can manage about five minutes. The Mayor couldn't manage three."

"I noticed you looked very absorbed. I envied you."

"I was thinking of girls," he said. "I always do at functions."

I had no reason to doubt him. Every morning I read the best Roman

126 *Rome as it looks today, seen from the Janiculum. In the distance are the Alban Hills.*

daily newspapers. Each of them, on page three, has an array of scholarly essays on history, on art, or archaeology and similar topics. They are very erudite. But the page, without fail, is illustrated by pictures of bathing beauties and juvenile film actresses.

"I find," I said, "I am growing a little tired of the past myself. Perhaps it's because in Rome there's so much of it."

He smiled. "It's my job to see that there's a good deal more. When anything is dug up, I go and see it. I'm supposed to stop it being destroyed."

"Have they discovered anything recently?"

"They discover something about once a week," he said, sipping sweet liqueur from a tiny glass. "More often than that, for all I know.

"Do you mean that they dig things up and don't tell you?"

"Certainly. The things that are dug up nowadays are nearly all tombs. If the building contractors told me, I'd have to preserve them. If the contractors had any sense of history, Rome would be one big graveyard. Fortunately, they haven't. Two years ago they unearthed a Christian catacomb. It was too big to hide, so we stopped the building operations. It was discovered in the foundation of what was to be an apartment block for re-housing the poor. Two hundred men were thrown out of work and fifty parents waited one year more to see the sun and air and sleep less than four in a room."

"What happened in the end?"

"That is an official secret." He changed the subject. "Where do you live in Rome?"

"In Old Rome, professor."

"I see. And you're bored with it?"

"At the moment, yes, very."

"I quite understand," he said. "It often bores me, too. When it does, do you know what I do?"

"You think of girls?"

"No. I get in my car and go for a drive round new Rome—the one they're building outside the walls. I think you will find it beautiful. I do. Don't tell anyone I said so or they'll think I'm a Philistine and I shall lose my job. But take my advice. Go and see it."

Some time later, very much by chance, I did.

The wind, I remember, had failed. It is called the *ponente,* and it determines the mood of Romans more than anything else—more than love, more than money, more than the news of the day, which few Romans think about unless it is scandalous. The *ponente* blows in the evening. It is a light wind and it comes trickling into the narrow

127 *Tourists still flock to Rome and the Romans still ignore them. But Tourist Boards and other authorities now make an effort to give them what the expect. In summer the principal monuments are floodlit, and in many ways a tour of them by night is more impressive than seeing them by day. Here is one of the most familiar outlines in the world, that of the Colosseum (the sloping right-hand edge, however, is not part of the original building, but a brickwork restoration).*

128 *The Sports Palace—a new covered arena designed by Pier Luigi Nervi. The dome is supported by an intricate web of Nervi's "pre-cast cement" and its diameter is more than double that of the dome of St Peter's.*

129 *The Flaminio Stadium—also designed by Pier Luigi Nervi. It holds 50.000 people.*

127

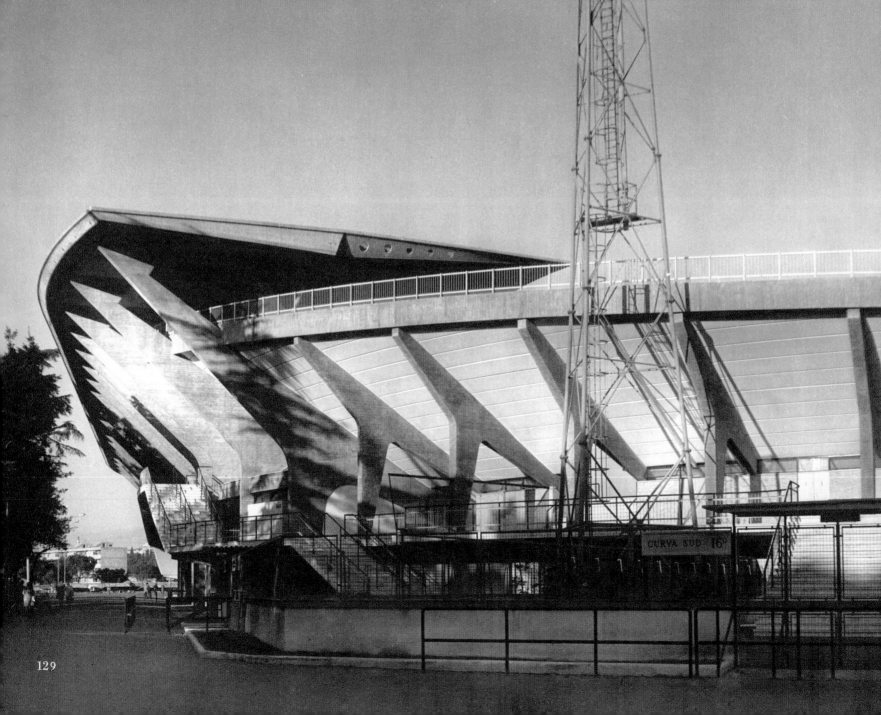

130

131

132

133

134

135

streets of Old Rome like a refreshing drink. The sun sets, the lights go on, and everybody save the bedridden and the people in gaol go out for a walk. You walk along the streets, you walk in the piazzas, you walk under the trees in the Pincian Gardens. You do not sit in cafés, unless you are imitating foreigners or are with elderly women. Coffee costs money and sitting still, for a Roman when out of his house, is a tremendous effort. He prefers to be on the move, to go from place to place, preferably without any purpose at all.

His mind, like the professor's, will be on girls, whom he will eye from head to foot. I do not know for sure what Roman women think about when they are strolling because I am too shy to ask, but I should imagine that, if they are girls, they reciprocate, and if they are married women I suppose they worry about the girls their husbands are looking at. I would, I know. In the early evening in Rome, unfaithfulness is in the air. There is a play of eyes, of glances, a slight turning of pretty heads that must be very disturbing to a mother of a family. For others, it is a delight.

A delight, that is, to be enjoyed only when the wind blows. When it doesn't, the game is off. The air grows heavy, one's step is less jaunty, the streets seem narrower than ever. The Roman men still eye the girls—I have seen them do it from doorways even in a cloudburst— but the girls look fierce and gaze straight ahead. At such times, I usually take my evening walk by the Tiber. On the evening that I am describing, I walked further along the banks than I had ever done before. I walked, as I thought, right out of Rome. The road ended abruptly at the gates of a gas-works. I turned off left and immediately I was lost. The neighbourhood was shabby, ill-lit and profoundly depressing, even, I fancied, when the *ponente* blew. I walked more quickly. I got more lost. But ahead of me I saw brilliant lights, surprisingly high in the sky. I made for them. In a few moments I came out of the slums into the Piazza of the Navigators. It is named after the Italian seamen, who discovered much of the New World. When I looked around me, I was almost as astonished as they.

The Piazza of the Navigators is a vast hemicycle of new buildings, perhaps a third of a mile across. The buildings are massive and run up to eleven stories. The centre building is crowned with a gigantic electric sign, the light that I saw in the sky. At the foot of these buildings runs an arcade, dazzling with more electric signs and brilliantly-lit shop windows. From the open side of the hemicycle runs a wide road, with many carriage-ways, that leads, after several miles, straight to the sea. On this evening, one side of it seemed a river of rubies, because it was filled with swiftly moving automobiles, while the other side ran with gold from their headlamps.

I had never seen it before. I told myself it could not be Rome. But I looked about me and there were Romans in the arcade, walking to and fro, doing nothing, eyeing the girls. And there was a breeze. It was not the *ponente*. It came, I suppose, up the wide road from the sea.

As the professor had foreseen, I found it beautiful. It was brash, but I was enchanted with the lights, the size, the spaciousness. I felt alive. I wondered if I had felt so alive in Rome since I came there. In the middle of the piazza that honoured the great discoverers, I had made a discovery myself. I thought this called for a drink in celebration, and I made for one of the bars. As I approached its chrome, glass and neon front my joy was completed. From out of the doorway came the thump and bounce of music from a loudspeaker, and it was playing the song that the errand-boy whistled under my window every morning.

I went in. The bar was shiningly clean. A tall pillar in the centre ran up to its high ceiling. On the sides of the pillar were ceramic reliefs, brightly coloured, making fun of the more portentous episodes of Roman history.

I examined the ceramics and decided that the Roman dignitaries in togas were perfect portraits of the Romans as I had discovered them to be. I went to the bar and ordered my drink. The bar-tender was polite enough to serve me, although, as I remembered, I should have bought a ticket at the cash-desk first. But I had almost never gone into such places. They disturbed, I had thought, my sense of history, so I had used restaurants.

Then I saw that the music was coming from a juke-box. I drank off my drink to give me courage and for the first time in my life I put a coin in one of these much-criticised machines.

I found that it was all very pretty. There are knobs, dials, twinkling lights, like some inaccessibly expensive toy that one saw as a child going Christmas-shopping. I found there was even a pane of glass to press my nose against.

But I am letting my memory run away with me. I did not, in fact, put my first coin in a juke-box with my own hands. I was much too stupid to follow all the instructions. A young boy next to me very kindly did the thing for me. He then asked me, with an apprehensive look, what tune I would like.

"That one that's just finished playing."

He beamed. I was delighted that my taste had been approved. Machinery turned, arms wove complicated patterns, and from a golden and silver grid worthy to be a screen in a Roman Emperor's palace, came my errand-boy's song.

The record, to my surprise, was in English. The voice was innocent, the sentiments most worldly.

"Bernardine," said the gold and silver grid, "Bernardine! Your separate parts are not unknown, but the way you assemble them's all your own."*

I laughed. Some ten Romans, men, boys, girls, standing round about me laughed too. When the record was finished, it occurred to me that it was most unlikely that any of them would have understood a single line of the song. The tune elated them, as it had elated me each morning when it woke me in Old Rome.

The boy at the knobs looked up at me, his dark eyes dancing. He had the round face and flopping curls that marked the Roman boy even in the times of the Renaissance.

"Enjoying yourself?"

"Very much. What's your name?"

"Nino."

"How old are you?"

"Thirteen."

"You look like a Roman. Are you?"

"Roman of Romans. My father is, too, and so's my grandfather."

He spoke proudly, as he should. Three generations of Romans is nowadays a long span to be able to boast of.

"Do you go to school?"

"No. I work in a filling-station."

"What are you going to be when you grow up?"

"A Teddy-boy."

He used the English phrase, to the delight of his listeners.

"Where did you hear that phrase, Nino?"

"We all use it here," said one of the listeners.

"But Nino, a Teddy-boy is a delinquent."

"Yes, I know."

"And you want to be a delinquent?"

"I'll have to be. My father says I'm going to grow up to be one, and he says I mustn't ever say he's wrong about anything."

"What are you going to do when you're a Teddy-boy?"

He brushed back the hair from his forehead. His black eyes grew intense with anticipated joys.

* Copyright by Johnny Mercer.

"Run around in gangs."

"Doing what?"

"Wearing blujins. My father won't let me wear blujins yet."

Blue jeans (the word is pronounced with neat Italian vowels) are slowly making their way in Rome. Boys wearing them are frowned upon by their elders.

"What crimes are you going to commit?"

His eyes sparkled.

"Play flippers."

Every Roman is unshakably convinced that Americans call pinball games "flippers". Playing at pin-tables is considered by the older generation a vice so terrible that they have succeeded in having them prohibited by the police. Clandestine clubs in cellars have sprung up where adolescents furtively tread the primrose path: for joy, not money, since the boys do not bet.

"You like American things?"

He frowned. "American?"

"Yes. Blue jeans are American. So are pin ... I mean flippers. That rock 'n' roll record you have just put on is an American tune."

He looked away. He gave a quick little yawn, a sign among Roman boys that one is talking nonsense to them. I realised then that, to him, since he had never known Rome without them, such things were Roman.

It was eleven o'clock. The barman told us it was time to go.

Outside the Piazza of the Navigators was still bustling with life. The great red sign still blazed. The cars were even thicker upon the road.

"I'm glad I lost my way," I said to Nino.

"Would you like to come again? I can show you the new houses. They're *belle ... belle ... belle ... belle!*"

"All right! When?"

"Sometime. When you're this way again. Goodnight."

I found a taxi. I drove into Old Rome. I stopped the taxi near my house, for I felt I wanted to stretch my legs before I went to bed. I walked a little, then I turned into the vast courtyard of the Borghese Palace. Fountains were playing. Great statues of Roman goddesses stood on plinths, buxom, broad-beamed and serene.

I stood in front of one of them, as I had done a hundred times before, admiring them. But the tune of *Bernardine* was running in my head. I hummed it. I thought of the words. Suddenly the goddess seemed very funny. I sang her a snatch of *Bernardine*. "Your separate parts are

137 *In the Campo dei Fiori, an open-air market in the very heart of Rome, once used for executions, the fish-woman is making a sign with her left hand to avert the bad luck which having her photograph taken might bring her. Such superstitions are fast dying out in a Rome where women drive cars, work in offices and go home each evening to watch television.*

138 *A young couple studying their map seem to be lost or perhaps facing the problem of getting from Piazza Navona to the Pantheon, a matter of only a few minutes for a Roman. The streets of Old Rome can be very bewildering, and one can easily lose oneself every hundred yards.*

139 *The Via Vittoria Veneto is the land of the big hotels and the smart cafés. This whole area was opened up for development at the end of the last century when the Ludovisi properties were sold: but only in these post-war years has the Via Veneto become the international centre of Rome.*

140 *Sitting in cafés in the street is not only for the rich. There are hundreds of small and inexpensive cafés and eating-houses with their tables and chairs in the open.*

141 *The Piazza of St Peter's, with its Bernini Colonnade, is a place that the Romans make good use of: and, although it is Vatican property, they look upon it as their own. Mothers bring their children to play: old men sun themselves and read their newspapers resting comfortably against a column and, on windy days, Romans drive their cars there to get a free wash-down from the spray of the fountains.*

142 *Here two Carabinieri patrol the Piazza of St Peter's. Although it is not Italian soil, but papal, the Italian State is responsible for law and order in the piazza.*

143 *A street-vendor selling arbutus-berries from his brightly-painted cart.*

138

139

140

141

142

143

144

not unknown, but the way you assemble them's all your own," I told her.

The policeman on guard moved towards me. He recognised me.

"Have you had a happy evening, sir?"

"Very, very happy, officer."

"A reception?"

"No. I've been seeing Rome."

"They say, sir," he remarked, sagely, "that there's always something you haven't seen in Rome, even if you live here a hundred years."

"There certainly is, officer," I said. "There certainly is."

I subsequently found that there is, in fact, something new to see in Rome every week. It is one of the fastest-growing cities in Europe. In 1939 it had a population of a million. Now it has two and a half. The Romans, though, like all Italians, they are not averse to begetting children, could not have produced this stupendous expansion by their own efforts. Other Italians have flocked to Rome from every corner of Italy, and the stream shows no sign of stopping. It has been calculated that, in all the city of Rome, only two hundred thousand people can, like Nino, really call themselves Romans.

I did not see Nino again until the Feast of St Peter and St Paul. On that day a gigantic fisherman's net is hung over the entrance of St Peter's. The Pope comes in wearing his tiara, but Romans stay away until he is gone. Then they take over the church. They come in thousands with their children. The children used to be held up to kiss the bronze toe of the statue of St Peter, but fewer and fewer do this now. New Rome has found a new game. The children are taken round the basilica and introduced to all the marble animals on the tombs of the pontiffs. They pat a lion's rump, they stroke a griffin's head. Does that, I wonder, happen in any other sacred place in the world?

Since I had never had the privilege as a child, I stroked and patted, too, when suddenly I saw Nino in the crowd. I waved. I shouted (you can, in St Peter's, on such days). He waved back and after a little pushing and elbowing, we met.

Nino gave a slight wave of his hand in the air. That is the fashion among the younger Romans. But he introduced me to the man who stood near to him. It was his father and he shook my hand in the stately manner of older Rome.

Nino's father was a broad-shouldered man, with his son's round face and lively eyes. The roughness of his hand in mine, the power of his shoulders told me that he was a manual labourer. Nothing else did. The Roman poise, Roman courtesy, Roman charm belong to all its

144 *The Termini Station's front-of-house appearance is considered one of the finest pieces of contemporary architecture. Designed by six young architects, it was started before the war, but finished only in 1950.*

145 *A section of the United Nations Organisation, the part that deals with food and agriculture, has its home near the Baths of Caracalla. This picture shows a part of the Conference Hall. A distinctive feature of many modern Italian buildings is the continued use of traditional arts and crafts, such as mosaics, ceramics and wood inlays. The last is seen in striking use in the bold design of the pillars here.*

citizens. Every class is well-mannered except, perhaps, the highest, which sometimes has no manners at all.

"My son said you wanted to see the new apartment blocks."

"Yes. He said they were beautiful."

Nino's father smiled with pleasure. He threw out his chest.

"They are. I built them myself."

A fussy verger making way for a priest in vestments through the crowd separated us for a while. Nino's father, who was tall, talked over the head of the priest.

"Why don't you come down and see it with me? Yes? Good! Today. Six o'clock." He gave me an address. It was in Garbatella, one of the most notorious slums of Rome.

I arrived on time. Garbatella is known throughout Rome as the haunt of thieves and loose women. It was a sordid network of streets lined with houses from which the plaster had in part fallen off. My taxi twisted and turned for a while, then pulled up outside a ruinous house with an iron fence round it. Some of the fence lay in a tangle on the ground. Outside this fence stood Nino, his father and another man. Their suits were worn, but neat and pressed. Plainly they were poor, yet they managed, as all Romans do, to look elegant.

The third man was introduced as Nino's uncle. He was in his thirties, and he was the most elegant of the three. I saw at once from his glance that he thought I was slumming from curiosity and he disliked me for it. He suggested that instead of going into the house, we went to the wine-shop.

The wine-shop was of the sort that is fast disappearing. It was low-ceilinged, it had wooden tables and benches and it served only the cheapest wine. But it was good wine. Even had it not been, the manners of Nino and his father were so graceful that it would have seemed so. Even the uncle lost a little of his suspicion after the first glass and warmed to me.

The wine drunk, Nino said:

"Now you must come home and meet my mother. My uncle doesn't want you to, because we're very poor and we all live in two rooms. At least, three, because I sleep in the hall. Still, you've got to come because Mother wants to see you."

The hallway was about ten feet square. Nino's bed stood vertically against the wall. The other two rooms were each about twelve feet square. In one of them lived Nino, his mother, his father and three children, one two years old, another five and another three. In the next room lived Nino's uncle and his young wife and their first baby.

Nino's mother greeted me cheerfully, her youngest child on her arm.

"I thought you'd like to see the worst," she said. "You couldn't get more crowded than this, could you? But we get along."

The rooms had almost no furniture save the beds. We stood in Nino's hall and talked. Then I noticed, on a shelf, a record-player and a small pile of records.

"That's Nino's" said his mother. "He bought it out of his own money. He hangs over it for hours. We call it his girl-friend."

"It's busted," said Nino. "But you can listen to the needle. It plays quite loud, especially when everything's quiet and they've all gone to bed."

He picked up a disc, absently. He looked at the broken record-player. He stood quite still for a moment and his eyes grew dark and wide. None of us spoke.

He tossed back his head, laughed and said:

"I bought it off another boy. What a swindler! But we are all crooks in Garbatella."

Everybody laughed. The uncle seized the moment to ease me out of the door. Nino's mother made her youngest say *ciao* and wave good-bye. We set out to see the new world round the corner.

On the way I said to Nino, "I'll get you a record of that tune we played on the juke-box."

"The one you liked? *Bernardine*? Thanks, but I've got it. It's one of my favourites, too."

I thought of Johnny Mercer's sophisticated words and music coming through the needle of the player at midnight, in Garbatella, and Nino listening, dreaming. I thought of all it must have meant to him in that cramped room. I wished that I did not write books for people to read, but songs for them to sing.

Nino's uncle was explaining something to me earnestly. I brought my attention back to him. They were bricklayers, he was telling me. They were very poor, but it wasn't always like that. When the new building started, bricklayers came in from all over Italy. The pay was good, when you got it. But there were many months, especially in winter, when nobody would hire you.

"Here we are," said Nino's father. "Now, what do you think of *that*?"

We stood on a slight rise. To our left, a quarter of a mile away, ran the brown walls of ancient Rome. In front of us, stretching away to the right, was a whole new city. It was made of great blocks of apartments, each block bright with balconies painted in different colours. We walked on further, entered the new city and passed down its wide new roads. The buildings had fine entrances, some lined with the beautiful marbles of Italy. The balconies were hung with flowering plants. Broad windows with coloured blinds let in the sun and air. People sat out on the terraces under awnings, watching the sunset.

"Ten years ago all this was waste-land," said Nino's father. "Just over there, where that building is, with the broad blue bands of tile round it, exactly where that is today was a sort of hollow. It was filled with hovels in which people lived. They were even worse off than we were. *Now* look at it."

Augustus, who boasted that he had found Rome brick and left it marble, could not have been more proud of his new Rome than Nino's father was of this.

"And over there," said Nino's uncle, "where you see they're building, is going to be a block for working-people like us. We've got our name down. We'll be in next year."

"If only," said Nino, with the dark distrust of thirteen years, "you and Father make enough money to pay the deposit."

"God willing," said Nino's father, "we shall."

I suppose a housing settlement of great concrete buildings does not come within the province of beautiful things. But to me, standing there and remembering Garbatella, it seemed more beautiful than the palaces that line my street. I thought so then. I have just got up from my desk and looked out of the window at Prince Ruspoli's palace and Prince Borghese's palace, and I think so still.

But on the day that I first saw new Rome—or a single part of it, for there are a dozen of these new Romes ringing the old city—there was one thing wrong with it. There were hardly any residents. There were a few people on the balconies and terraces. They were mostly elderly. It was plain that all the apartments were inhabited, but nobody came in or out of the marble entrances and the brand-new streets were deserted.

I asked Nino's father about it.

"Well," he said, "today's a national holiday, you see."

"I know," I said, "but wouldn't that mean that more people than usual would be at home?"

"Twenty years ago," said Nino's father, "you *had* to stay at home on a holiday, otherwise Mama or Grandmama would be offended. Now nobody does, unless they're ill."

Nino looked down a road wistfully. He pointed to the west.

146 *Physically a part of Rome, though legally a sovereign state, the Vatican comprises some hundred and ten acres of gardens, palaces and churches, including St Peter's. It was set up by the Concordat of 1929 between the Italian State and the Pope, which was an attempt to solve the problem of the Pope's temporal power. It is part of the Concordat that the authorities in Rome do not permit anything to go on which would do harm to the reputation of Rome as a sacred Christian city. The clause is frequently invoked by the Vatican against such things as indecorous clothing, improper films and plays, and irreverent publications. The authorities sometimes take action, and sometimes they do not.*

"They've all gone to Ostia," he said. "I was going too, but we hadn't any money in the house, as it happened, so we went to church."

"They're about due back now," said Nino's uncle, once more embarrassed. "Let's stroll about for a while and watch."

We strolled. We went into a bar. I returned the hospitality that had been offered to me, and we watched. Ostia is the nearest seaside to the city, and about seven o'clock the return from the beaches began. It is an astonishing sight.

The roads slowly fill with hundreds upon hundreds of small family cars, mostly all alike. Packed into each are families of six or seven, bronzed, in beach dress, and inebriated with hours under the Mediterranean sun. They wave, they shout, they sing the latest songs. The cars stop at their houses and they tumble out, clatter up the marble staircases, pour into their apartments, fling open the balcony doors and come out on to the terraces to snatch the last pleasures of the day.

"And over there," said Nino's father, "is the Cristoforo Colombo."

The Cristoforo Colombo is a wide arterial road with six lanes of traffic that runs from the Piazza of the Navigators straight to the sea. It is the Tiber of modern Rome. The Tiber has lost its romance for the contemporary Roman. He barely mentions it, and then only in connection with traffic jams and suicides by drowning. But the six concrete ribbons of the Cristoforo Colombo have won his affection and engaged his pride.

The lanes on the far side of the dividing strip were filled with returning cars. The one that led to the sea was empty. A fast car making an evening trip to Ostia shot past us.

"Wow-aah!" said Nino, imitating its noise. He gazed after it, his eyes gleaming. "If only I could go in a car like that."

The very next week he did, because I took him. In the months that followed I hired every sort of car. I took Nino to Ostia, I took his father, his uncle, his mother, Nino's friends and my own. I no longer walked along the Tiber when the *ponente* failed. I rang the garage. Within fifteen minutes I was at the gates of Rome. In eighteen minutes more I saw the sea. Two more minutes and I was at Ostia. Rome has become a city by the sea.

Old Ostia is a stretch of ruins that nobody I know goes to see. I pass it, usually at ninety miles an hour. New Ostia is a rabble of concrete buildings. Architecturally, it is a disaster. No Roman cares. Old Rome has the finest architecture in the world, and it is precisely that from which he wants to get away. New Ostia is ugly, vulgar and alive.

But, in any case, you do not stay there. You bathe, you eat sea-food, clamber back into the car and spin further along the coast. There are great pine woods that once belonged to kings. I have been shown their delights by Nino and his friends. I have hunted wild asparagus and taken it to a restaurant, had it cooked and eaten it with melted butter. I have picked the prickly red fruit they call a sea-cherry and tasted its strange blend of the sweetness of fruit and the bitterness of the sea. I have hunted rabbits, watched the sky flat on my back under a pine-tree. I have startled lovers. For young Romans, the pine woods are more part of the city than the Forum, in which most of them have never set foot.

I have even been to the rocky promontory called San Felice Circeo: it is known as the Capri of Rome, but it is not, thank heaven, like Capri at all, except for the shape of its mountain. Everybody runs away from Rome, but some refined and expensive people find Ostia too coarse. They go to a hotel by the sea in San Felice where they can sunbathe, water-ski, and in the evenings dance, secure that nobody will be in the hotel but their own sort. I explored this hotel a little. It is well-appointed: and I was charmed to find that the refined Roman dances to the music of a juke-box. It was just an ordinary juke-box. Nobody had thought of adapting the mechanism to make it four times as expensive. Rich and poor alike pay fifty lire for a tune.

The Cristoforo Colombo and the regular exodus has changed the whole Roman way of life. The road, and others like it, were completed just at the time when Italian engineers had applied their resourcefulness to methods invented by Henry Ford, and produced vehicles which even the ordinary Italian could afford to buy. They produced the tiny automobile which is called the Mouse (the *topolino*), they produced the family car that costs little to run, and above all they produced the motor-scooter which almost everybody in regular employment can afford.

Motoring immediately became a passion. The Roman, as I have said, does not like to sit still. Here was a means of keeping on the go beyond his dreams. He has even found a way of looking at the girls while he drives. He drives slowly beside her (the only time he will drive slowly in the course of his trip), makes a Roman remark, and speeds off before she can slap his face. As an example, for those whom it may interest, I may quote a friend of mine, who selects women who are plentifully endowed and remarks, in the politest of voices: "Young lady, tell me, does all that belong to you?"

The modern Romans are having a great deal of fun. But they periodically empty Rome. The result is that Rome is the one capital city in Europe or America with only the vestiges of a theatre. There are very few of them. They are open intermittently and they have been left to the intellectuals, who have succeeded in driving out even the customers who, not yet having bought a motor-car, still kept up the habit of theatre-going. The cinemas are so badly hit that in the summer most of them close down completely, while on a fine day in winter (and Rome has many) they are barely a third full. The opera, which used to depend on the well-heeled middle-class, is now resigned to living off the foreigner. The third night at an opera is the cheapest. The modest Roman music-lover used to fill the theatre. It is now the modest tourist. The music-lovers are all by the sea, or driving in the country, loving music by means of transistor radios.

Perhaps the greatest change that Henry Ford and modern road-making machinery has brought about is in the social life of Rome. The capital has been, for centuries, the seat of the greatest families of Italy. They had their own way of living, which largely consisted in impressing the rest of the Romans that they had an aristocratic disdain for money. But the great families were great landowners, and land, especially near the old limits of the city, has grown to be immensely valuable. The princes and princesses have dropped their well-bred disdain for cash (since there is so much to be made) and are rapidly turning themselves into landlords and landladies. I do not know what the Roman nobility talked about before the change. But I am told that it was the latest fashion from Paris, the latest shows in London, horses, hunting, marriage and adultery. They also had a continuous flow of private witticisms which were quite unamusing except to themselves. From my experience among them in Rome today, their conversation consists in the rental values of seaside villas, how to raise buildings by a storey to accommodate more people and what so-and-so said to such-a-one about where the new arterial road was really going to be built.

I recall inviting a Countess to a dinner-party. She once was one of the best conversationalists I have known. She came straight from her lawyers. She was dressed for dinner, but she clutched a large file of documents. No sooner had she sat down than she opened the file and began talking of a vexing lawsuit about one of her houses that she rents. She talked about it till we went to the restaurant where we were to eat. I noticed that her file had disappeared. I wondered, for a moment, where it had gone, because we had walked straight from the taxi to the table. When we rose to go I found that she had been sitting on it.

I think the upper stratum of Roman society will adapt itself to the new middle-class Rome of outings to the sea, small cars and suburbs. Indeed, I know it will. There is a restaurant to which I sometimes take visitors. It is a place where the gilded youth of Rome gathers in the evening. A short while ago an Italian who had returned home after many years in South America asked the guitarist to play some of the old Italian songs. The guitarist obliged with a heart-breaking song about somebody's Mama. The returned Italian sang it, in a sweet tenor. The young men all took out their handkerchiefs, buried their faces in them and heaved their shoulders as though they were moved to uncontrollable tears. The Roman is an excellent clown when he chooses: he is proud of the fact. The song died away. The returned Italian fell silent. The guitarist struck up another song which the young men greeted by cheering. It was not *Bernardine,* but it was an excellent Italian imitation of it.

Rome was not built in a day, but the bigger part of it was built in the last twenty years. New Rome is not in the guide-books. All that side of Roman life has no interest for the new Roman at all. Thousands of them do not come to the centre of the city for months on end. New Rome is building its own suburban life, a more vigorous, more happy, more healthy way of living than Rome has known for centuries.

For the visitor who comes to the city to see only its ancient monuments, I know that new Rome is an intrusion and a disappointment. But he should see it: he will gain a better comprehension of why the men who built the older city built as they did. It should be remembered that the romantically beautiful Spanish Steps were a piece of development. They were put up to replace a patch of wasteland surrounded by hovels that had persisted through the centuries. The Piazza del Popolo was deliberately designed to make a grand finale to one of the roads that lead into Rome, precisely as the architects of today have designed the Piazza of the Navigators. The Imperial Forums, whose vast ruins are still noble, replaced the slums of a place called, in classical times, the Suburra. The sweeping colonnades of Bernini before St Peter's were a piece of town-planning that was intended to liberate the basilica from a warren of nondescript buildings, two of which remained down to the days of my boyhood. In the very heart of the city, under the Capitoline Hill, are the ruins of a Roman apartment house, a relic of another time when the population of Rome was bounding upwards. The Via Giulia, the street in Rome most evocative of the past, was in fact a piece of planned urban development initiated by a pope who detested the crooked streets and

149 *It is customary for the popes to mark great events in the Church with ceremonies of great magnificence, following which St Peter's and Castel Sant'Angelo are illuminated with "fiaccole"-iron bowls of tallow with large wicks that burn for hours on end, whose origins probably date back to medieval, if not Roman, times. Here is the Castel Sant'Angelo on the night of the promulgation of the Dogma of the Assumption in 1950.*

149

airless buildings of the city which he ruled. Some part of Rome has always been new.

As for Old Rome, there is talk of banning traffic from it and making it a sort of historical reservation. If they do, my apartment will be very quiet, which is a good thing for a writer. As for me, I shall move: probably to Ostia.

I shall, in a word, do as the Romans do: for Rome, to them, is not old at all, but young.

150 *St Peter's and the Bernini Colonnade illuminated on the same occasion. Note in the background on the right the light in the top-floor window. This is the Pope's private library, the room from which he also blesses the crowds which gather in the piazza.*

151 *The Chair of St Peter in the sumptuous setting provided for it by Bernini. The actual chair is within the one shown in this picture and is of the type that Roman senators were accustomed to use when being carried about Rome. The pagan empire, its conversion to Christianity, the growth of the power of the popes, the ebullience of the Counter-Reformation, and the permanence of the Catholic Church and its continuity are all thus summed up in this magnificent shrine for a sedan-chair.*

100 Pietro da Cortona: *Church of Santa Maria della Pace, Rome*
Commissioned 1565
Photograph Georgina Masson

101 Diego Velasquez: *Pope Innocent X*
1650. Oil on canvas. 140 × 110 cm.
Doria Pamphili Gallery, Rome
Photograph O. Savio

102 *Doria Pamphili Palace: Dutch Salon*
Decorated 18th century
Photograph D. Lees

103 *Doria Pamphili Palace: Venetian Salon*
Decorated 18th century
Photograph D. Lees

104 Anonymous artist: *Tournament in the courtyard of the Belvedere*
16th century. Engraving
Rome Museum
Photograph Alinari

105 Anonymous artist: *Papal benediction in the Piazza of St Peter's*
18th century. Oil on canvas
Prince Borghese collection, Rome
Photograph Gabinetto Fotografico Nazionale, Rome

106 Giovanni Battista Piranesi: *Back façade of Santa Maria Maggiore*
18th century. Engraving
Department of Prints, National Gallery, Rome
Photograph Georgina Masson

107 Giovanni Battista Piranesi: *Piazza di Spagna*
1750. Engraving
Department of Prints, National Gallery, Rome
Photograph Georgina Masson

108 Giovanni Paolo Pannini: *Pope Benedict XIV arriving at Santa Maria Maggiore*
1742. Oil on canvas. 265 × 253 cm.
Quirinal Palace, Rome
Photograph O. Savio. By courtesy of the Segretariato Generale della Presidenza della Repubblica

109 Giovanni Paolo Pannini: *Piazza Navona flooded*
1756. Oil on canvas. 95·5 × 137 cm.
Landesgalerie, Hanover
Photograph O. Savio

110 Auguste Caron: *Augustus and the Sybil on the Capitol*
c. 1566. Oil on canvas. 125 × 170 cm.
Louvre, Paris

111 Paolo Posi: *Monument for the Feast of St Peter and St Paul, 1752*
1752. Engraving
Rome Museum
Photograph Gabinetto Fotografico Nazionale, Rome

112 Anonymous artist: *Fountain of Trevi*
18th century. Oil on canvas
Count Giambattista Spalletti Trivelli collection, Rome
Photograph Gabinetto Fotografico Nazionale, Rome

113 Nicolo Salvi and others: *Fountain of Trevi* (*detail*)
Finished 1762
Photograph Georgina Masson

114 Gaspard van Wittel (Vanvitelli): *The Forum from the Capitol*
1683. Tempera on parchment. 23·2 × 43·7 cm.
Palazzo Colonna collection, Rome
Photograph Gabinetto Fotografico Nazionale, Rome

115 Anonymous artist: *Group of Englishmen at Rome*
1749-52. Oil on canvas. 89 × 132 cm.
The Hon Mrs Ionides collection, Buxted
Photograph Gabinetto Fotografico Nazionale, Rome

116 Giovanni Paolo Pannini: *Views of modern Rome*
1757. Oil on canvas. 167·5 × 244 cm.
Boston Athenaeum, Boston, U.S.A.
Photograph Gabinetto Fotografico Nazionale, Rome

117 Giovanni Paolo Pannini: *Piazza Navona*
1729. Oil on canvas. 110 × 250 cm.
Louvre, Paris
Photograph Gabinetto Fotografico Nazionale, Rome